ECONOMIC COMMISSION FOR EUROPE
Committee on Environmental Policy

ENVIRONMENTAL PERFORMANCE REVIEWS

BULGARIA

Second Review

UNITED NATIONS
New York and Geneva, 2000

Environmental Performance Reviews Series No. 11

NOTE

Symbols of United Nations documents are composed of capital letters combined with figures. Mention of such a symbol indicates a reference to a United Nations document.

The designations employed and the presentation of the material in this publication do not imply the expression of any opinion whatsoever on the part of the Secretariat of the United Nations concerning the legal status of any country, territory, city of area, or of its authorities, or concerning the delimitation of its frontiers or boundaries.

UNITED NATIONS PUBLICATION
Sales No. E.01.II.E.5
ISBN 92-1-116773-6 ISSN 1020-4563

Preface

A first Environmental Performance Review of Bulgaria had been undertaken in 1995 as a joint project between UNECE and OECD. In September 1999, the UNECE Committee on Environmental Policy agreed to the Bulgarian request for a second review by UNECE. The project was the first second-round review of the EPR programme in a country in transition. The conceptual framework for such second reviews had been discussed by the EPR Expert Group and agreed by the Committee on an earlier occasion.

The structure as well as the organizational details of the project were decided towards the end of 1999, taking the results of the first EPR project as well as the considerable changes that had occurred in Bulgaria in the meantime into account. The review team included national experts from Denmark, France, Germany, Italy and Ukraine, together with the UNECE secretariat. Part of the review expenses were covered by extrabudgetary funds that had been made available by Germany and Italy. These contributions were essential to the implementation of the project.

The review mission to Bulgaria took place in April 2000. The draft of the EPR report was then finalized and submitted to a Peer Review by the UNECE Committee on Environmental Policy at its annual session in Geneva on 27 September 2000, at which the Committee approved the recommendations as they are set out in this report. A delegation from Bulgaria, led by the Minister of Environment and Waters, assisted the Committee in its deliberations.

The review of Bulgaria, being a second exercise, follows a different approach than other environmental performance review projects. A broad overview of the developments since the first review is followed by assessments of the problems encountered – and solutions sought – with regard to five more narrowly defined priorities for Bulgarian environmental management. The reviewing experts presented a large number of practical suggestions to the national experts working in the respective fields, which, it is hoped, will be of value to them when seeking improvements in their management practices.

The UNECE Committee on Environmental Policy and the UNECE review team wish the Bulgarian Government success in their important future tasks, including the implementation of the recommendations contained in the present report.

LIST OF TEAM MEMBERS

Mr. Andreas KAHNERT	(ECE secretariat)	Team Leader
Ms. Catherine MASSON	(ECE secretariat)	Project Coordinator
Mr. Andreas KAHNERT	(ECE secretariat)	Chapters 1 and 2
Ms. Catherine MASSON	(ECE secretariat)	Chapters 1 and 2
Mr. Arne JACOBSEN	(DENMARK)	Chapter 3
Mr. Stefan DOYTCHINOV	(ITALY)	Chapter 4
Mr. Henri HORNUS	(FRANCE)	Chapter 5
Mr. Heinrich SPIES	(GERMANY)	Chapter 6
Mr. Vasyl PRYDATKO	(UKRAINE)	Chapter 7

The review mission for the project took place from 10 to 14 April 2000, and the Peer Review was held in Geneva on 26 September 2000. The UNECE Committee on Environmental Policy adopted the recommendations as set out in this publication.

Information cut-off date: 27 September 2000.

TABLE OF CONTENTS

LIST OF FIGURES

LIST OF TABLES

LIST OF BOXES

ABBREVIATIONS

AAQ	Ambient air quality
BDCS	Biological Diversity Conservation Strategy
CBCP	Cross Border Cooperation Programme
CBD	Convention on Biodiversity
CFC	Chlorofluorocarbon
CITES	Convention on International Trade in Endangered Species of Wild Fauna and Flora
CoP	Conference of the Parties
EE	Environmental expertise
EEA	Executive Environmental Agency
EIA	Environmental impact assessment
ELV	Emission limit value
EU	European Union
GEF	Global Environmental Facility
GHG	Greenhouse gas
GIS	Geographical information system
GTS	Globally threatened species
ISPA	Instrument for Structural Policies for Pre-Accession
MAF	Ministry of Agriculture and Forestry
MEPF	Municipal Environmental Protection Fund
MEW	Ministry of Environment and Waters
MoE	Ministry of Economy
MoF	Ministry of Finance
MRD	Ministry of Regional Development and Public Works
NARDP	National Agricultural and Rural Development Plan
NBCP	National Biodiversity Conservation Programme
NEHAP	National Environmental Health Action Plan
NEPF	National Environmental Protection Fund
NESDC	National Environmental and Sustainable Development Centre
NGOs	Non-governmental organizations
NNPS	National Nature Protection Service
NSI	National Statistical Institute
NTEF	National Trust Eco-Fund
ODS	Ozone-depleting substances
PA	Protected Area
PEBLDS	Pan-European Biological and Landscape Diversity Strategy
PEEN	Pan-European Ecological Network
PHARE	Assistance for Economic Restructuring in the Countries of Central and Eastern Europe
REC	Regional Environmental Centre
REI	Regional Environmental Inspectorate
SAC	Special Area of Conservation
SAPARD	EU Special Accession Programme for Agriculture and Rural Development
SPA	Special Protected Area
UNDP	United Nations Development Programme
UNECE	United Nations Economic Commission for Europe
USAID	United States Agency for International Development
VOC	Volatile organic compound
WWTP	Waste-water treatment plant

Currency

Monetary unit: Lev (plural leva)

Exchange rates: The Bulgarian National Currency, the lev, was pegged to the Deutch Mark (DM) in July 1997: 1000 Leva for 1 DM

Year	1 US$
1994	0.07
1995	0.07
1996	0.49
1997	1.78
1998	1.68
1999	1.76
2000*	1.83

Source: International Financial Statistics, IMF, 1999

Note: Values are period averages

PART I: EVOLUTION OF ENVIRONMENTAL POLICY AND MANAGEMENT FROM 1996 TO 1999

Chapter 1

LEGAL, POLITICAL AND INSTITUTIONAL FRAMEWORKS

1.1 Major policy orientations and management practices

Integration into the European Union

In 1997, Bulgaria decided to seek integration into the European Union (EU) and following this decision took a number of preparatory steps that clarified the long-term development perspectives of the country. Since then, Bulgaria has been accepted as a candidate for accession to the EU and, in anticipation of accession, institutional as well as organizational arrangements have been made in the Bulgarian Government itself. At present, the preparatory work for EU integration is focused on assessment of the costs of accession as well as on the sources of funding.

The Council for European Integration at the Ministry of Foreign Affairs comprises 15 of the 16 Bulgarian Ministers, while the Committee for European Integration is made up of Deputy Ministers. These bodies were constituted to prepare the future negotiation process and to oversee 30 working groups, serviced by the Central Coordination Unit (see below), dealing with the various management areas involved in the accession process. Environmental issues are the responsibility of Working Group 22 which is composed of representatives of 11 ministries as well as participants from social groups, including non-governmental organizations (NGOs), and has also set up a number of subgroups. Its main task is to review all legal instruments to ensure their conformity with relevant EU regulations and directives. Prior to submission of a legal instrument by the Ministry of Environment and Waters (MEW) to the Council of Ministers, and possibly to Parliament, the approval of Working Group 22 is required.

At the expert level, the Central Coordination Unit was created at the Ministry for Regional Development and Public Works as part of the Special Preparatory Programme for the EU Structural Funds for Bulgaria. The Unit includes representatives of all ministries and State agencies and coordinates the sectoral programmes of the National Development Programme 2000–2006. In addition to the 30 working groups mentioned above, the Unit is empowered to create inter-ministerial working groups, eight of which are currently functioning. In addition, intra-ministerial working groups exist in all participating ministries. The results of the Unit's work require approval by the institutions of the Ministry of Foreign Affairs, mentioned previously. The Unit also collaborates with UNDP and the World Bank on integration issues relevant to their respective programmes. In general, however, its work is seen as a starting point for inter-ministerial collaboration, which otherwise does not appear to have an established institutional framework.

The Department for European Union Integration in the MEW has a staff of eight. This Department prepares decisions on subjects affecting the environment, adjusting Bulgaria's legal instruments prior to EU accession and determining their priority. The strategy followed in the revision of laws consists of incorporating EU requirements strictly. When necessary, the door is, however, left open to allow for extension of an initial period of 'soft enforcement', which is determined in cooperation with the industries concerned. When questions of interpretation of EU legislation arise, the Department seeks guidance from the European Commission (DGXI) or the EU delegation in Bulgaria. Analogous departments exist in other ministries which collaborate when aspects of EU legislation make it necessary. This applies mainly to the ministries of agriculture and of industry. Cooperation is coordinated by Working Group 22 and if conflicts arise between ministries, they are submitted for resolution to the Deputy Ministers of the ministries concerned.

Bulgaria benefits from twinning projects in many areas. The MEW's main twinning partner is Germany, followed by Austria and France. Ten projects were included in the 1998 programme. Preparation of the 1999 programme is going ahead, while development of the 2000 and 2001 programmes is envisaged. The main immediate task is seen to be the elaboration of a new Governmental environmental strategy, as the most recent version dates back to 1994, and did not receive Government approval.

Current overall priorities for environmental policy

The environmental strategy developed in 1992 was adopted by the Government, and its update in 1994 resulted in a ministerial programme that determined the main priorities of the country for the period up to the year 2000. Lessons learnt from the previous strategy are reflected in the updated one. It also set guidelines for action, and the implementation of the measures included in the strategy will soon be completed. With assistance from Germany, a new national environmental strategy is being developed which will include an action plan of work to be completed before the end of the year 2000 following approval by the Council of Ministers. Prior to its submission, all environmental institutions, local authorities and NGOs will be able to review the draft and make proposals for amendment.

The strategy includes sectoral programmes on air, water, waste, chemical substances, soil, noise, nature protection and radiation. In addition, inter-sectoral influences on the environment by the energy, transport, agriculture, metals and chemicals industries are described, and suggestions made for the solution of problems. Finally, consideration is given to the contribution that may be made to the solution of environmental problems by the Ministry of Health.

The development of closer cooperation between the institutions concerned with these sectors and the MEW is seen as a task for the future. At present, of the two existing inter-ministerial working groups, one is to make provisions for the phasing out of leaded petrol. It is headed by the Executive Agency of the MEW and, in addition to the administrations involved in the issue, includes representatives of the two major national refineries. The other working group, chaired by a Deputy Minister of the MEW, is to prepare implementation programmes for new environmental legislation passed during the approximation process to the EU. At present, inter-ministerial cooperation is organized primarily on an ad hoc basis and in relation to specific issues. Examples are the determination of tax rates between the MEW, the Ministry of Finance and the

Ministry of Transport, pursuant to the provisions of the Law on Fuel Taxes, and the national coordination for the ISPA programme with the Ministry of Regional Development and Public Works.

The development of local and regional programmes for environmental protection is well under way, the first three programmes involving the Pernik, Stara Zagora and Vratsa regions and dealing primarily with waste management issues. They are to be approved by the MEW, which bases its waste management activities on regional programmes. The absence of satisfactory horizontal cooperation between municipalities is hampering the development of joint waste treatment and disposal installations. The MEW encourages cooperation between municipalities in this area by according funding priority to joint solutions. In addition, meetings are arranged between municipalities on issues such as ISPA requirements or waste-water treatment.

Environmental management in the privatization process

Agricultural land in Bulgaria had not been nationalized, but was owned by cooperatives. Thus, instead of being privatized, it was restored to its previous owners, who may or may not have formed new cooperatives. The restitution process was managed by the Ministry of Agriculture and has been completed. No special environmental considerations were involved in the restitution process beyond those set out in general environmental legislation.

The privatization of industry began following the adoption of the Privatization Law in 1992. The privatization of small and medium-sized enterprises (within the competence of the sectoral ministries) is now virtually complete. A Privatization Agency was created for the privatization of larger enterprises (i.e. enterprises valued in 1995 at 1 million or more Deutchmarks. Any privatization proceeds were paid directly into the State budget. In 1995, in accordance with World Bank methodology, a list of enterprises slated for privatization was established, and each year, plans for privatization are approved by Parliament. Four hundred of the approximately 520 larger units are now privately owned and in the year 2000, the range of companies offered for privatization - or partial privatization - is being extended to include public utilities like energy, transport, water supply and sewerage companies, which have hitherto been excluded.

Environmental policy objectives are included in the industrial privatization process at a prominent level. In fact, no other sectoral policy concerns are singled out in the privatization process and the final purchase contracts. There was no major objection to the scheme from the business sector, as enterprises see environmental improvements of production as a necessary precondition for their commercial integration into western Europe. The MEW is mandated to implement the related provisions within the privatization procedure with a view to (a) encouraging remediation of environmental damage caused by the enterprise prior to privatization, and (b) concluding a phased programme with new owners for full compliance by the enterprise with current environmental norms and standards. Different instruments are applied to the management of each of these objectives, but consistency is achieved through an underlying environmental impact assessment (EIA). In other words, an EIA is undertaken together with an analysis of past damage, and an environmental audit.

The new environmental legislation in Bulgaria holds the State liable for past environmental damage from enterprise activities. The extent of the damage is determined by a special analysis for each enterprise undergoing privatization. The assessment follows the Methodological Guidelines for the Scope and Content of Past Environmental Pollution Reports in the Privatization Process, approved by the Minister of Environment and Waters. The preparation of the scheme involved notably a 1997 pilot project in connection with the privatization of a copper smelting plant, which was financed through a World Bank credit and a Swiss grant. Each special analysis gives rise to a remedial plan and the determination of a ceiling for the funds deemed necessary to repair the damage. The remedial plan, including the time frame within which repair is to be carried out and the limit on funding, is built into the privatization agreement. Remedial measures are then undertaken by the enterprise, but funded from the State budget up to the set financial limit. Depending on the situation, the amount may be paid from the environmental fund, but credit arrangements for the purpose, totalling 50 million US dollars, have also been negotiated with the World Bank.

Regarding the second objective, compliance with norms, an environmental audit of the enterprise is undertaken. It identifies the existing compliance problems and forms the basis for a plan to be implemented by the enterprise, at its cost. This compliance plan is also contained in the privatization agreement. It specifies the measures that are required in order to assure conformity, and may specify a time schedule for staggered implementation. It is too early to draw conclusions regarding the application of the scheme. In the initial phase, the remedial plan and the compliance plan were not always ready before the purchase contract was signed, but it is believed that in the near future this problem will disappear.

1.2 Legal and institutional developments

Legal instruments

The revision of the Environmental Protection Act (EPA), adopted in September 1997, was the principal development in environmental legislation during the four years 1996 to 1999. This revision incorporated some earlier decrees (EIA, auditing, certification of experts) into the central environmental legislation. It also adapted EIA procedures to the updated EU Directive, specified new possibilities for EIA by local authorities, created environmental inspectorates at the local level with NGO participation, and considerably stiffened sanctions, including fines, in cases of violation of the legislation.

Following the revision of the EPA, new regulations were prepared, as follows:

- Regulation No. 4/1998 on environmental impact assessment (EIA), specifies the EIA procedures provided by law and brings Bulgarian legislation to full conformity with EU practice. Bulgaria has also ratified the Convention on EIA in a transboundary context. In 1998 the Convention was incorporated into the national legislation, making possible the participation of other countries in the procedure. The effective participation of the public in decision-making is also part of EIA procedure. The public hearing begins as soon as the documentation is complete and ends before the final decision is made. The public has a possibility of pressing for the consideration of alternatives, or for a complete halt to the procedure. In the years 1997-1998, projects for an incinerator for chemical wastes were rejected by the public and NGOs, both in Asenovgrad and in Sofia. A flow diagram of the EIA process is shown in Figure 1.1.

Figure 1.1: The scheme of the EIA procedure in Bulgaria

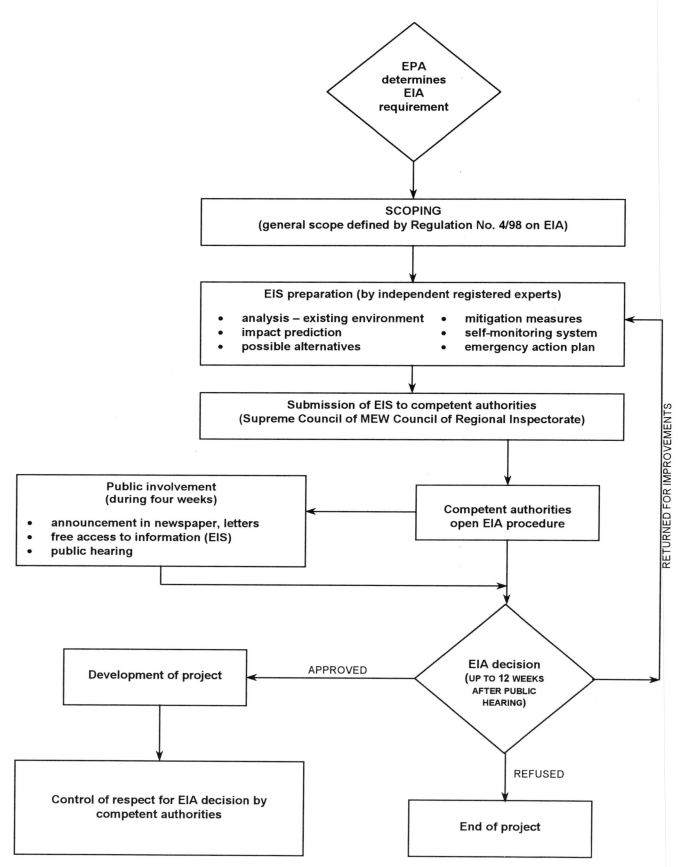

- An amendment and supplement to the regulation on sanctions for exceeding limits to environmental contamination and damage were promulgated.

- The regulation regarding collection of environmental information and access to such information was redrafted into a new legislative act.

New legal instruments were enacted with regard to all aspects of environmental protection: air, water, waste, protected areas and mineral resources.

The *Clean Air Act* of June 1996 sets out a legal framework for air management that is adapted to the transition period. It defines the responsibilities at all administrative levels in the country. It introduces permitting regimes, and specifies procedures that will lead to the gradual introduction of industrial emission standards. In the year 2000 the Act has been amended to achieve full compliance with the requirements of the EU Framework Directive on Air Quality (96/62/EC), by introducing new AAQ parameters and defining mechanisms to achieve improvement in areas of non-compliance.

The following implementing regulations have been enacted or are in preparation:

- Regulation on emission measurement from stationary sources. The regulation provides for enterprises carrying out their own measurement of emissions in accordance with the European standards for AQ and the implementation of EU Directives

- Clean Air Act and its amendments (SG 45/96, am. SG 85/97, am/ SG 27/00)

- Regulation 14 of 23 September 1997 on the maximum permissible concentrations of harmful substances in urban air (SG 88/97)

- Regulation 1 of 13 February 1998 on the terms and conditions for adopting temporary air pollution emission limit values from existing stationary sources (SG 51/98)

- Regulation 2 of 19 February 1998 on adopting emission limit values (flue gas concentrations) for pollutants from stationary sources

- Regulation 3 of 25 February 1998 on the terms and conditions for adopting temporary emission limit values for pollutants from existing stationary sources, related to the national combustion and energy balance (SG 51/98)

- Regulation 7 of 1999 of the Ministry of Environment and Waters and the Ministry of Public Health on air quality assessment and management (SG 45/99); (Directive 96/62/EC)

- Regulation 8 of 1999 of the Ministry of Environment and Waters and the Ministry of Public Health on ground-level ozone standards (SG 46/99); (Directive 92/72/EC)

- Regulation 9 of 1999 of the Ministry of Environment and Waters and the Ministry of Public Health on emission limit values for sulphur dioxide, nitrogen dioxide, particulate matter and lead (SG 46/99); (Directive 99/30/EC)

- Regulation 6 of 1999 of the Ministry of Environment and Waters on the terms and conditions for measuring emissions of pollutants from stationary sources (SG 31/99)

- Regulation 15 of 1999 of the Environment, Industry, Regional Development and Health Ministries on emission limit values (flue gas concentrations) of sulphur dioxide, nitrogen dioxide and particulate matter, emitted in the air by major new stationary combustion sources (SG 73/99); (Directive 88/609/EEC)

- Regulation 16 of 1999 of the Environment, Industry, Regional Development and Health Ministries on the reduction of volatile organic compounds emissions from petrol transportation, storage, loading and unloading operations (SG 75/99); (Directive 94/63/EC)

- Regulation 17 of 1999 of the Ministry of Environment and Waters and the Ministry of Public Health on standards for the content of lead, sulphur and other environmentally hazardous substances in fuels (SG 97/99); (Directives 9/32/EC and 98/70/EC)

- Regulation on industrial and hazardous waste handling and transportation (SG 25/99) – under the Waste Management Act; (Directive 94/67/EC)

- Regulation 11 on the conditions for erecting and operating facilities for household wastes decontamination (SG 10/99) under the Waste Management Act; (Directive 89/369/EEC)

- Decree of the Council of Ministers 12/99 on the regime for placement of hazardous substances (SG 4/99)

- Decree of the Council of Ministers 254/99 on the control and management of substances that

deplete the ozone layer (SG 3/00) ensuring the implementation of Regulation 3093/94/EC
- Regulation 5/98 on the issuing of permits for import, export and transit of hazardous waste (SG 120/98)
- Regulation 4 on environmental impact assessment procedures (SG 84/98)

The foregoing harmonization of domestic laws on air with the EU Air Quality directive completed the approximation of the Framework Directive - 96/62/EC and the new European Directives on Air Quality assessment and management. However, the immediate implementation of all new provisions would be beyond the current financial possibilities of industry.

The new *Water Act* was adopted in July 1999 and entered into force in January 2000. The adoption of the Water Act was part of the implementation of the first stage of the Strategy for the Integrated Management of Waters in the Republic of Bulgaria adopted by the Council of Ministers on 17 November 1997. The Act sets in motion the implementation of many activities envisaged in the various stages of the Strategy. The new Water Act is in line with the EU legislation, but now requires a series of implementing regulations as the management by hydrographic basin is not yet effective (see Chapter 5).

The Water Law still requires a series of regulations to be formulated, in particular on the discharge of harmful substances into waste waters and into receiving water bodies, and concerning discharge permits, protection from nitrate pollution, etc. The quality of drinking water, and of bathing water, should also be regulated. Corresponding implementing acts have been prepared and are in the process of adoption in order to achieve the entry into force and effective implementation of the Water Act:

- Methodology for determining the minimum acceptable flow in rivers;
- Regulation on the investigation, use and protection of groundwater;
- Regulation on the quality of drinking water;
- Regulation on the qualitative requirements for the surface waters intended for the municipal drinking-water supply;
- Regulation on the protection of waters from pollution by nitrates from agricultural sources;
- Regulation for the conditions and the order for investigation, designing, approval and

operation of sanitary protection zones around water sources and installations for the municipal drinking-water supply and around the sources of mineral waters used for medical, drinking and hygiene needs;
- Regulation on the quality of waters for bathing;
- Regulation on the quality of waters for breeding fish and shell species;
- Regulation on the quality of coastal marine waters;
- Regulation on the procedure and the method for determining discharge limits for industrial waste waters into municipal sewerage systems;
- Regulation on the emission limits and the admissible concentration of harmful and dangerous substances in waste waters that are discharged into bodies of water;
- Regulation on the issuing of permits for the discharge of waste water into bodies of water and determining the individual emission restrictions for point sources of pollution;
- Regulation on the procedure and the method for establishing the networks and the operation of the National Water Monitoring System.

The *Law on the Reduction of Harmful Impact of Waste on the Environment* was passed in September 1997. The Law applies to industrial, construction, and domestic waste, and to hazardous waste, including hospital waste. The collection, storage or disposal of wastes requires a permit. Hazardous waste will be collected and stored separately. All sites where hazardous waste is generated or disposed of are subject to an EIA. This new umbrella law also regulates information flow, waste movement, controls and sanctions. The Law calls for the elaboration of a National Waste Management Programme - achieved in 1999. The Law rules that the construction of solid waste facilities will be financed by the State budget. Overall, the Law and Programme are in line with the EU legislation, in particular directives 75/442/EEC, 91/689/EEC and the Community Strategy COM (96) final. Particularly noteworthy is the creation of new economic tools for an active waste management, such as charges for products whose production or consumption processes are environmentally unfriendly, and tax concessions for waste treatment facilities.

About 11 statutes subsidiary to the Law have been prepared. They cover waste classification, and permits for import, export and transit of waste, and define the obligations of the State under the Basle Convention. Also covered are the need for reporting on waste management activities, requirements for construction and exploitation of installations for municipal solid waste disposal, requirements for waste treatment facilities, requirements for construction and exploitation of waste landfills, and conditions for the granting of permits under the Law on the Limitation of Adverse Effects of Waste on the Environment. Requirements for transport and treatment of industrial and hazardous waste were also adopted, as well as a tariff on charges for tyres in application of the Law on the Limitation of Adverse Effects of Waste on the Environment.

The *Law on Protection from the Harmful Impact of Chemical Substances and their Processing* is before the National Assembly. The Law was elaborated in accordance with EU Directives on the classification, packaging and labelling of dangerous substances, on restriction of the marketing and use of certain dangerous substances and preparations, on classification, packaging and labelling of dangerous preparations, on good laboratory practice and on the evaluation and control of the risks of existing substances.

The *Law on Protected Areas* was enacted in 1998 and revised and completed in March 2000. It regulates the protection of biodiversity through the conservation of habitats within a network of protected territories. It also regulates the management of protected territories through specialized structures, specific management plans and reinforcement measures for the conservation of species of wild birds.

Regulations on the preparation of management plans for protected areas are also being drafted, in order to:

- Regulate activities in State-owned protected areas.

- Renew tariffs for authorized activities in protected State-owned areas (regulation already adopted) and for compensation in cases of damage caused to protected areas. The charges for collecting medicinal plants from State-owned land, forests and water have been reduced by between 30 and 70 per cent in the Tariff on Charges, which was approved by the Cabinet. The reduction of charges concerns a large number of widely distributed types of medicinal plants and wild mushrooms in State forests. Lowest are the charges for collecting

flowers of colt's foot and elder, respectively 0.03 and 0.02 leva. Those for blackberries and raspberries are 0.15 leva and for 1 kg of mushrooms, they are between 0.22 and 0.28 leva. The charges for roots, root systems and tubers are retained unchanged, as their collection destroys the plants and creates erosion. The Cabinet approved the charges for using water sources in protected areas. For the local population, the charges for pasture and timber are the same as those under the Forestry Act. The charges for collecting wild fruit in the protected areas also remain unchanged between 0.02 and 0.15 leva/kg, and between 0.30 to 1.30 leva per animal for pasture.

- Elaborate and implement rules for the structure and operation of State Park Directorates (approved by the MEW in 1999).

In 1997, the *Law on Plant Protection* was adopted. Amendments to this law are currently (May 2000) under discussion in the Council of Ministers. A new Law on Hunting and Protection of Wildlife Act was approved by the Council of Ministers in March 1999 and was under consideration by the National Assembly in December 1999. Until its enactment, the 1982 Law on Hunting remains in force. New acts are currently in the Council of Ministers such as the Law on Biodiversity, the Law on the Black Sea Coast, the Law on the High-Mountain Zone, and the Law on Fishing and Aquaculture.

The new *Law on Medicinal Plants* was approved by Parliament in November 1999. There is no law on genetically modified organisms, but the need to draft the Biological Safety Act was mentioned in NBCP, 2000. Bulgaria signed the Protocol on Biosafety in Nairobi, during CBD-COP-5. In addition, a Genetically Modified Organisms Bill is intended for discussion in the National Assembly in June 2000. At the present time, such organisms may be imported and used without restriction.

Since 1997, the Government has worked out and implemented the following legislative initiatives: Restitution of Forests and Forestland Law, Forestry Law, Hunting and Fishing Law, Law on Amendment and Supplement of the Concession Act. The main priorities include accelerating the restitution of private forest and land of the forest fund, achieving a balanced management and operation of the State and private forests, separating regulatory and management functions in forestry, etc.

The European legislation on nature protection, and on biological diversity in particular, consists of six directives and regulations, whose requirements have been partly transposed into Bulgarian legislation. Full harmonization is expected by the end of 2000, following the adoption of the Law on Biological Diversity. The MEW drafted the concept and the structure of this law in 1999. It will be the first document in Bulgarian legislation to clarify such notions as "ecological corridor", "core areas", "buffer zones", Natura-2000 and Emerald network, etc. These activities are proceeding, while, on the other hand, Bulgarian (unlike European) legislation does not yet regulate:

- The protection of bird habitats outside protected areas
- The catching, killing, or trading of specific bird species
- Procedures for the protection of species (of Regulation 338/97/EEC) falling outside the range of the CITES Convention
- Procedures, forms and other import/export-related documents included in Regulation 338/97/EEC, which are different from those under the CITES Convention
- Procedures and accompanying documents for the control of trade, acquisition, possession and movement within the country of representatives of the species under Regulation 338/97/EEC
- Customs offices where the import/export is carried out
- Procedures for the sale of confiscated species inside the country.

Some actions have been taken to improve urban territories and landscapes. On 22 July 1999 the Council of Ministers approved the *Territorial Planning Bill*, which regulates construction activities in urban areas and the country as a whole. The new statute superseded the 1973 Regional and Urban Planning Act and simplifies procedures for assigning, drawing up, coordinating and approving planning schemes and their changes.

The new *Underground Resources Act* has been in force since March 1999. It regulates prospecting for, exploration of, and production of underground resources, together with their rational utilization and the protection of the subsurface. Its full implementation is possible since the adoption of the following legal instruments:

- Tariff of application fees for prospecting and/or exploration permits and for concessions for

mining mineral resources (in force since July 1999)
- Tariff of annual area fees paid by holders of permits for prospecting and/or exploration of mineral resources (in force since July 1999)
- Regulation on the principles and methods for determining concession payments for mining of underground mineral resources in accordance with the Underground Resources Act (promulgated in June 1999)
- Regulation on the geological and technical documentation of exploration and mining sites (promulgated in December 1999)
- Regulation on preparing and maintaining the National Balance of Reserves and Underground Resources, the Specialized Register of Deposits and the Register of Discoveries (promulgated in December 1999)
- Regulation on a Unified Register of Prospecting and/or Exploration Permits (promulgated in December 1999)
- Regulation on the National Geo-Fund (promulgated in January 2000)

The existing *legislation on noise* includes specific requirements, economic mechanisms and regulators that need to be updated and brought into line with European legislation. The development of the draft Noise Act and related by-laws has been interrupted pending promulgation of the corresponding new EU Framework Directive.

Overall institutional arrangements

The current Ministry of Environment and Waters was set up in 1997, bringing much of the national environmental management under one ministerial administration. The former Ministry of the Environment, the National Water Council and the Geology Committee were thus merged. The present structure of the Ministry of Environment and Waters is shown in Figure 1.2.

The Ministry is responsible for:

- Developing and implementing national policy in the environmental sector; preparing the legislative and regulatory basis in the areas of water, ambient air quality, waste, nature protection, chemicals, noise, accidental discharges into the environment and risk of industrial incidents; horizontal legislation; adapting of legislation to that of the European Union

Figure 1.2: Structure of the Ministry of Environment and Waters

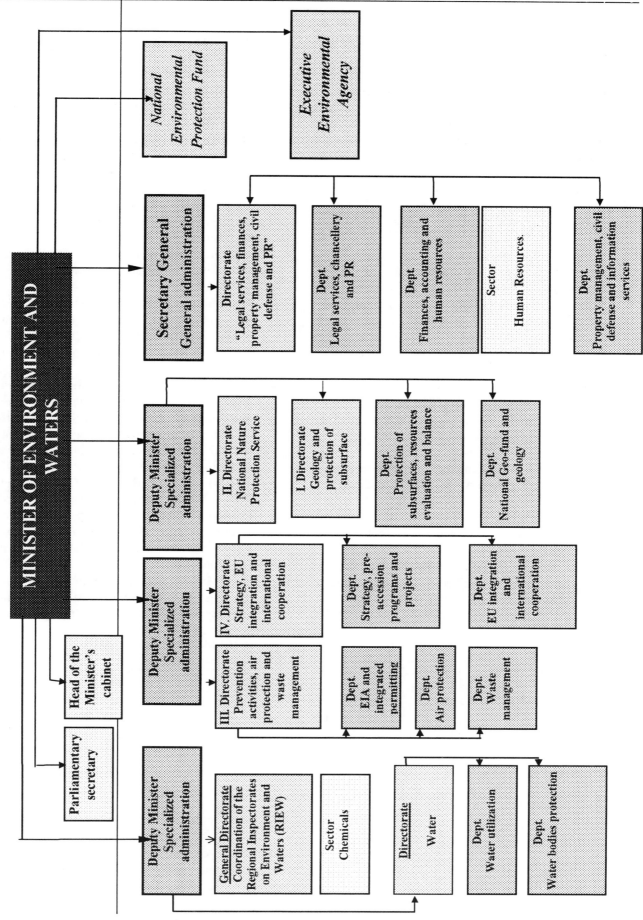

- Managing protected areas which are exclusive State property
- Allocating and protecting water resources
- Issuing permits for use of natural and mineral resources and taking decisions on the environmental impact assessment results for large industrial plants and activities of national importance.

Under the Ministry of Environment and Waters, 15 Regional Inspectorates for Environment and Water have been established. Their main functions include:

- Controlling the implementation of and compliance with environmental legislation
- Supporting municipalities in the preparation and implementation of local policy for environmental protection
- Informing the public about the state of the environment
- Issuing decisions on environmental impact assessments for sites and activities of regional importance, and issuing permits for industrial activities and waste treatment facilities.

The Executive Environmental Agency is an administrative body within the framework of the Ministry of Environment and Waters. It:

- Manages the National System for Environmental Monitoring;
- Carries out monitoring activities and laboratory analyses of air, water, soils, wastes, noise, ionizing and non-ionizing radiation;

- Supervises the Regional Environmental Inspectorates and is responsible for the quality of the received data;
- Collects, processes, stores and publishes information on the state of environmental components; and
- Develops periodical issues and an annual bulletin of the state of the environment.

The Executive Environmental Agency is a reference centre in Bulgaria, in the framework of the European Environment Agency.

Other State bodies, responsible for aspects of environmental protection are:

- The Ministry of Health monitors the impact of the ambient and working environments on human health, determines the State disease prevention policy, for example, regarding the quality of drinking water.
- The functions of the Ministry of Agriculture and Forests include the protection, restoration and maintenance of soil fertility, the protection of water from contamination with agricultural nitrates, and the use and protection of forests, including those in protected areas.
- The Ministry of Regional Development and Public Works implements national policy on territorial planning and public works, is responsible for water supply and sewerage, and formulates the National Plan for Regional Development.
- The Ministry of Transport prepares norms limiting harmful emissions from transport vehicles and controls their implementation.

Figure 1.3: Environmental management across ministries and major institutions

Competent environmental authorities	*Other relevant institutions*
↓	↓
Ministry of Environment and Waters	State bodies responsible for environmental protection • Ministry of Health • Ministry of Agriculture and Forests • Ministry of Regional Development and Public Works • Ministry of Transport
Regional Inspectorates	
Executive Environmental Agency	Local administration/municipalities
	State bodies supporting environmental protection State Agency for Use of Atomic Energy for Peaceful Purposes State Agency for Energy and Energy Resources State Agency for Energy Efficiency State Agency for Standardization and Meteorology

Specialized State bodies contributing to the solution of environmental problems are:

- The State Agency for Use of Atomic Energy for Peaceful Purposes, which is a regulating body in the area of nuclear safety and radiation protection.
- The State Agency for Energy and Energy Resources elaborates programmes for the development of the energy sector, and particularly for the reduction of environmental pollution from energy-related activities.
- The State Agency for Energy Efficiency devises and promotes policies for effective and rational use of energy and the use of alternative energy sources.
- The State Agency for Standardization and Metrology harmonizes Bulgarian State standards with international and European standards for environmental management.
- The National Institute of Statistics collects and processes statistical information on the state of the environment and industrial pollution.

The system of environmental management embracing the ministries and other major institutions is presented in Figure 1.3.

International cooperation

Until the end of 1999, the International Cooperation Department was responsible for bilateral cooperation and accession programmes, the Projects Department for PHARE projects, and the Strategy and Economic Regulatory Department for the overall coordination of international projects. Since January 2000, the Strategies, European Integration and International Cooperation Directorate has been responsible for all these activities.

During the period 1996-1999, Bulgaria ratified the following international environmental conventions, protocols and amendments:

- The Convention on Biological Diversity on 29 February 1996, paving the way for the elaboration of the National Biodiversity Strategy (1998).
- The Convention on the Conservation of Migratory Species of Wild Animals and its three related Agreements (on the Conservation of African-Eurasian Migratory Waterbirds, on the Conservation of Bats in Europe and its

amendments, and on the Conservation of Cetaceans of the Black Sea, Mediterranean Sea and Contiguous Atlantic Area) in 1999.

- The Basel Convention on the Control of Transboundary Movement of Hazardous Wastes and Their Disposal, on 18 January 1996. Bulgaria also ratified its amendments. It is now envisaging training customs officers in chemicals control. Under the Convention, obsolete pesticides were sent for treatment to the Netherlands, as Bulgaria did not have adequate facilities. With the implementation of its national waste management plan, Bulgaria will soon have a treatment centre and landfills for hazardous waste management. The identification and analysis of hazardous waste will be improved.
- The Vienna Convention for the Protection of the Ozone Layer and Montreal Protocol, on 5 January 1997, the London and Copenhagen Amendments on 13 May 1998, and the Montreal Amendments on 23 September 1999. The World Bank is helping to finance a project aiming at phasing out the production and consumption of ozone-depleting substances in seven Bulgarian enterprises. The cost of the project amounts to 13.5 million US dollars.
- The Danube Convention on 23 March 1999.
- The VOC Protocol to the UNECE Convention on Long-range Transboundary Air Pollution on 27 February 1998.

Bulgaria signed other international legal instruments:

- The Kyoto Protocol to the United Nations Framework Convention on Climate Change, on 11 December 1997. At the fourth Ministerial "Environment for Europe" Conference, in Aarhus, Denmark (June 1998), Bulgaria signed the Declaration of the Ministers of Environment in the Region of the UNECE, the Convention on Access to Information, Public Participation in Decision-making and Access to Justice in Environmental Matters, and the 1998 Protocol on Heavy Metals and 1998 Protocol on Persistent Organic Pollutants to the Convention on Long-range Transboundary Air Pollution.
- The Protocol to Abate Acidification, Eutrophication and Ground-level Ozone to the Convention on Long-range Transboundary Air Pollution, in December 1999.

- The Protocol on Water and Health to the Convention on the Protection and Use of Transboundary Watercourses and International Lakes, in June 1999.
- The Charter on Transport, Environment and Health, in June 1999.

Bilateral agreements and protocols on environmental protection have been concluded with a number of countries:

- Agreement on Environmental Cooperation between the Government of the Republic of Bulgaria and the Government of the Republic of Turkey, signed in Ankara on 28 July 1997. No common project has been developed so far, although possibilities for cooperation in transboundary protected areas are being explored.

- Agreement between the Ministry of Environment and Waters of the Republic of Bulgaria and the Ministry of Environmental Protection, Natural Resources and Forestry of the Republic of Poland, on Cooperation in the Field of Environmental Protection, signed in Warsaw on 26 November 1997.

- Agreement between the Ministry of the Environment and Waters of the Republic of Bulgaria and the Ministry of Housing, Spatial Planning and Environment of the Kingdom of The Netherlands on Cooperation in the field of Environmental Protection, signed in Amsterdam on March 31, 1998. A joint-implementation project in the town of Pleven has been concluded with the Netherlands. Another step was signed for DM 2.5 million on 10 April 2000 for another such project, modernizing monitoring systems in the cities of Pravetz, Varna and Sofia.

- Agreement on Environmental Cooperation between the Government of the Republic of Bulgaria and the Government of the Russian Federation, signed in Moscow on 28 August 1998.

- Agreement on Environmental Cooperation between the Government of the Republic of Bulgaria and the Government of the Kingdom of Denmark, signed in Sofia on 14 June 1999.

- Protocol between the Ministry of Environment and Waters of the Republic of Bulgaria and the Ministry of Environment of the Slovak Republic, signed in Bratislava on 18 May 1999.

- Protocol between the Ministry of Environment and Waters of the Republic of Bulgaria and the Environment Protection Agency of Ireland, signed in Sofia on 3 July 1999.

- Protocol between the Ministry of Environment and Waters of the Republic of Bulgaria and the Ministry of Waters, Forests and Environmental Protection of Romania, signed in Sofia on 23 November 1999. An intergovernmental commission was set up early in 2000 to resolve the problem of transboundary air pollution by industrial facilities along the Bulgarian-Romanian border. Audits of industrial plants are conducted jointly on both sides of the border, and solutions will be worked out in cooperation.

- There is also a bilateral agreement with Greece under which a common monitoring system for the River Struma was set up in 1999, with assistance from the PHARE programme.

- A memorandum of understanding focusing on air protection was recently concluded with Italy.

Bulgaria has thus concluded bilateral environmental agreements with almost all its neighbours. Among its next objectives is the conclusion, in the year 2000, of an agreement with the former Yugoslav Republic of Macedonia, and the re-establishment of cooperation with Yugoslavia through the Balkan Stability Pact. It is expected that this will help resolve an acute environmental problem on the Timoc river, polluted by heavy metals from Yugoslav mining activities (Bor mines), while the river water is used downstream in Bulgaria, particularly for irrigation purposes. Among further Bulgarian objectives is the improvement of cooperation with donor countries of western Europe.

Environmental projects and foreign aid

In 1998, the Ministry of Environment and Waters supervised the implementation of 41 projects with international financial participation. Eleven new projects were launched in 1998 while 5 were completed. Projects exist in the fields of water protection (11), air protection (2), solid waste management (3), biodiversity protection (4), environmental legislation (4), and other areas (3). The projects involve either institutional reinforcement (22) or investment (19). In 1997 and 1998 two donor meetings in the field of Bulgarian environmental protection were held to review current projects, financed by different donors. On these occasions the Ministry of Environment and Waters listed its priorities, and outlined its activities and the national programmes in the field of water and waste management, as well as selected project proposals requiring financing.

1.3 Integration of environmental objectives into enterprises and sectoral developments

General integration instruments aiming at enterprises

EIA, environmental audits and environmental management are the cornerstones of the integration of environmental objectives into enterprise activities in Bulgaria. The law on EIA was among the earliest legislation in the transition period and was modelled on the relevant EU directive (85/337/EEC). Its application revealed the need for a precise list of activities subject to EIA requirements that was adapted to Bulgarian circumstances. The list was refocused in 1997, so that four years' experience of a full application of modern EIA is now available in the country. Implementation of EIA is adapted to changing circumstances every two years, the last regulation in this regard dating to 1998. EIA decisions are taken both at the national level (by the Council of the Ministry), and at regional level (by the 15 Regional Councils and the Regional Inspectorates).

From the beginning, the EIA process included a permitting system that is not normally found elsewhere. The EIA decision for existing facilities specified permitted levels of pollutant emissions as the basis for environmental inspections. The repetition of EIA procedures at five-yearly intervals for all enterprises subject to EIA was also envisaged. Current intentions are to modify this requirement through a new protection law, in the course of the transposition of the IPPC Directive of the EU.

Also since 1996, the Environment Ministry has developed a national programme for environmental audits of enterprises. The environmental audit is carried out by licensed experts and is paid for by the enterprise. It examines the current environmental performance of the enterprise or plant and proposes a plan to bring its operation into compliance with relevant emission limits. The conclusions imply a programme of investment in cleaner technologies and waste reduction.

Compliance plans set specific temporary norms that apply to enterprises during the period until regular standards can be achieved. ISO 14001 was adopted as a national standard in 1998, and four enterprises began the voluntary introduction of environmental management.

The experiences with EIA as well as with environmental audits have had two major effects. First, they increased MEW's confidence that the IPPC Directive of the European Union could be implemented at an early date. It is currently envisaged to begin issuing integrated permits regularly as of 2003, for both new and existing enterprises. At present, integrated permits are being introduced on a pilot basis for six enterprises. Secondly, EIA and environmental audits have been included in the privatization procedure for industrial enterprises, enabling past environmental damage to be assessed together with compliance requirements (see section 1.1).

From 1996 to 1999, the Ministry of Environment and Waters issued 81 EIA decisions, including 19 assessments of past environmental damage. During the same period, the 15 Regional Councils issued 373 EIA decisions, including 15 assessments of past environmental damage (one in each Regional Inspectorate).

Sectoral integration and cooperation

Regional development and public works. The most complex cooperation between the MEW and the Ministry of Regional Development and Public Works (MRDPW) concerns water management. Responsibility for the development of investment programmes regarding the supply of drinking-water as well as for public sewerage are in the hands of the MRDPW, while the MEW is responsible for programmes involving allocation of water resources, waste-water treatment and monitoring. This responsibility also extends to any administration prior to the actual investment, i.e. tendering etc. The effective implementation of investment in these areas is the task of the MRDPW. Once waste-water treatment facilities have been constructed, ownership falls to the local administration concerned, which therefore becomes responsible for any privatization. Contact between the two ministries is usually maintained by correspondence, but for specific problems working groups may be set up. The national coordination institution for the ISPA programme is the MRDPW.

Cooperation between the two ministries is also required with regard to regional and local development. At present, there are 28 districts with regional development plans that may include substantial environmental protection sections. The Regional Inspectorates are heavily involved in the preparation of the plans, but there is no formal mechanism for this. The trend in the evolution of regional administrative authority is towards a gradual devolution of responsibility to the regional level. The biggest practical difficulty lies in the fact that routines for direct cooperation between local authorities are slow to emerge. While all authorities have in the meantime established the required waste management plans, only four have proceeded with the elaboration of a comprehensive environmental protection programme. The MEW assists actively in the development of local comprehensive protection programmes in various ways, including through the training of inspectors. The environmental fund accords priority to the financing of regional projects. Assistance is also provided by the REC in Bulgaria and by USAID. The situation is considered satisfactory for the time being, but it is expected that municipal administrations will soon require consulting assistance.

Health. In June 1998, the Bulgarian Council of Ministers approved a National Environmental Health Action Plan (NEHAP) for the period 1996 to 2000. Its preparation had been organized by the Centre for Hygiene, Medical Ecology and Nutrition, for the Ministry of Health, lasted for about two years, and involved NGOs, the general public, and governmental agencies. Its approval by the Council of Ministers enabled all ministries to provide input, in accordance with standard practice. The contribution of the MEW, however, did not extend beyond this routine procedure. At present, the NEHAP is in a process of updating, which should be completed by the end of the year 2000. Experts from both the MEW and the Ministry of Health hope and expect that cooperation between the two ministries in the NEHAP updating exercise will intensify, as in future all substantive departments of the MEW will be concerned with NEHAP implementation.

Another area of possible cooperation between the two ministries is that of monitoring and the use of monitoring data. Since 1997, monitoring has been integrated into the MEW. However, obtention of the necessary data by the Ministry of Health is not without cost. The Ministry may therefore decide to re-establish its own monitoring procedure and thus revert to the situation existing before 1997. At present, a regulation on access to information is under preparation in the MEW. It is planned to assure ministries of free access to the public information necessary in the pursuit of their functions. The Ministry of Health fervently hopes that such a provision will eventually not only be included in legal instruments, but will also be enforced.

Cooperation is also required on several other clearly defined issues. Some environmental hot spots in the country are characterized by high heavy metal concentrations in the ambient air. The collection of hospital wastes has been regulated since 1998, but serious problems exist regarding their treatment, and some population groups are often exposed to substantial health risks on or around landfills. Regarding drinking water, health risks are related to high nitrate concentrations as well as to microbiological pollution.

Energy. A Law on Energy and Energy Efficiency was enacted in July 1999. It created three agencies responsible for energy questions, which are represented in the Council of Ministers by the Minister of Economy and Trade. The State Energy and Energy Resources Agency develops action plans for the energy economy, in which the MEW is participating – at the present stage mainly by correspondence. An earlier energy development plan included a chapter on environment, but had not benefited from special input by the MEW prior to the routine coordination procedure for submissions to the Council of Ministers. The Agency is currently preoccupied with the restructuring of the energy sector in connection with the privatization programme. Cooperation with the MEW occurs primarily in relation to individual projects, often internationally supported.

The State Energy Efficiency Agency is preparing the regulations to implement the 1999 law. Active cooperation with the MEW has begun in connection with joint implementation projects, as foreseen by the Kyoto Protocol, in partnership with the Netherlands. Increased and more systematic cooperation between the MEW and this agency is envisaged regarding improvement of energy efficiency – a domain where it is considered that there is a need for substantial progress to be made. Such cooperation will also cover the promotion of renewable forms of energy, which is part of the Agency's mandate.

The State Energy Regulatory Commission has only recently started its work, and cooperation with the MEW has not yet had the time to develop.

In this as in other areas, steps have been taken to encourage closer cooperation between the public administrations concerned. In this case, the energy and environmental commissions of the Bulgarian Parliament jointly discussed issues of common concern. The high sulphur content of coal burnt for electricity generation – and the corresponding desulphurization of power plant exhaust fumes, the decommissioning of closed uranium mines, the substitution of cleaner fuels for coal in residential heating, the excessive energy intensity of Bulgarian industrial production, and the promotion of the use of unleaded petrol (approached through the creation of an inter-ministerial working group; unleaded fuel continues to be more expensive than leaded fuel), are some of the issues of common concern to environmental and energy management.

Agriculture. The Ministry of Agriculture and Forestry (MAF) has a special unit, the Ecology Department, which cooperates regularly with the Ministry of the Environment. Links maintained through the EIA units with the soil protection department of the MEW are particularly strong. In late 1998, the MAF, MEW and NGOs worked together on a concept for a sustainable development strategy. In 1999, a National Agricultural and Rural Development Plan (NARDP) for 2000-2006 was formulated under the EU Special Accession Programme for Agriculture and Rural Development (SAPARD) aiming at bringing agriculture and agro-environmental policies into conformity with EU requirements of the *acquis communautaire*. The NARDP was developed and coordinated under the responsibility of the MAF. Local people were consulted and the Plan was also submitted for comment to Ministries, in particular the MEW. The latter insisted on the necessity of including an environmental dimension in the monitoring of agricultural activities. It also sought to take part in the implementation of measures to be developed, and insisted that the minimum environmental requirements under each measure should be based on an EIA. The importance of complementarity and synergy between the different NARDP measures was also emphasized as soil erosion, acidification, salination and pollution, for example, were preoccupations common to several different parts of the Plan.

The NARDP includes a measure for the development of environmentally friendly agricultural practices, which will benefit from priority access to SAPARD funds. This is designed to counterbalance the negative impact of past monoculture that led to alterations in soil composition, soil acidification, soil erosion, diminished biodiversity, and soil pollution by pesticides, etc. The measure is intended to encourage farmers to turn to environmentally friendly agricultural production methods. Pilot projects, directed at certain environmentally sensitive areas, will be launched under the MAF and between 2001 and 2006, 12 million euros will be devoted to the scheme.

While there is a will to develop best agricultural practices, there are no guidelines so far. An initiative of the Academy of Agriculture in Plovdiv promotes organic farming and farmers can be trained on a model farm, which has also developed a certification system. But at the present time there is no real consumer demand for organic produce, and thus little incentive for the farmer to turn to organic farming methods.

Cooperation between the Ecology Department of the MAF and the department of soil protection of the MEW has intensified over the two past years. In particular, the rehabilitation of agricultural soils polluted by heavy metals provides opportunities for common action, in which, during soil monitoring, the Executive Environmental Agency also becomes involved. Recently, a regulation for the protection of water against nitrate pollution from agriculture was drafted by an interministerial Ad Hoc working group with the participation of the MAF, MEW and MH.

Cooperation between the two ministries MEW and MAF can be qualified as close, and is likely to intensify as a result of the arrangements planned under SAPARD. Also the intention to work together to prepare guidelines on best agricultural practices and a related certification system is to be encouraged. However, it seems that the protection of forests which is entirely under the MAF even in protected areas, has not been subject to concerted policy so farand the MEW has not been involved in the development of sustainable practices in forestry.

Economy. The Ministry of Economy includes a seven-staff unit responsible for coordination with the MEW. In addition to numerous well-defined projects– such as those designed to improve the production processes of major polluting industries – cooperation also extends to the general priority areas of the Ministry of Economy. For example, this Ministry arranged the World Bank loan of 50 million US dollars to remedy past environmental damage from privatized enterprises (see section 1.1 above). Another priority for joint implementation is the effort to increase energy efficiency in industry.

Transport. The Ministry of Transport and the MEW cooperate primarily to harmonize legal instruments (e.g. those concerned with emissions from transport vehicles), as well as the application of EIA to infrastructure enterprises. The transport of hazardous substances and the use of proceeds from fuel taxation also give rise to cooperation, as does the planned phase-out of leaded petrol. The Ministry of Transport has also recently established formal contact with the MEW aiming at closer cooperation.

Tourism. There is virtually no cooperation in this area between the Ministry of Economy, which now deals with industry, trade and tourism issues (MoE) and the MEW. The MEW relies entirely upon the EIA procedure to mitigate negative effects of the possible development of tourist infrastructures in the country, as each particular tourism project is subject to an EIA. There is so far no Law on Integrated Coastal Management, but the different environmental laws (on water, air, nature protection, protected areas, waste, etc) offer safeguards to protect the coast from infrastructure projects. Also, municipal territorial plans that are compulsory are subject to a strategic environmental assessment. Finally, should the management of a beach be placed under a concession regime, an environmental analysis is preliminary to any decision of the municipal council. All these instruments can be used to forestall mass tourism, which is not in the strategy of the country. Nevertheless, the National Development Plan foresees some tourism development and will be an instrument for coordination between the two ministries, once it has been adopted by the Government.

There is no national policy to foster sustainable tourism, and so far, eco-tourism has not been promoted by the MoE. Nevertheless, it has benefited from an initiative developed by UNDP when encouraging strategies for sustainable development. As farming does not bring in sufficient income in many rural regions, the combination of ecotourism and ecofarming activities is seen as offering an opportunity to maintain the rural population in place. A pilot project has been financed by UNDP in which two

municipalities, Asenovgrad and Velingrad, were chosen in a mountainous region. Their potential for ecotourism had been identified, entertainment arranged and the programmes advertised to potential Bulgarian customers. Results are expected in summer 2000. The objective is to build on the experience to include other villages. The MEW encourages ideas and projects on ecotourism and provides funds for marking eco-trails. The development of eco-tourism could be enhanced by increased cooperation between MoE, MAF, MEW and NGOs, and the possible support of UNDP.

1.4   Conclusions and recommendations

Since the first Environmental Performance Review, Bulgaria has considerably clarified its general political perspectives. Integration into the European Union has become its principal objective and it has set in motion a comprehensive adaptation process. Environmental policy and management have undoubtedly benefited from this extensive renewal of social orientation. But over and above achieving improvement of its status in this general reconsideration of social values and mechanisms, the Ministry of Environment and Waters has clearly applied considerable energy to upgrading its role in the country. As a result, despite the economic crisis, environmental policy objectives seem to have gained recognition in the society at large. The Ministry also appears to be playing a more significant role in the national administration, as can be seen from its presence in the industrial privatization process.

Of course, such dynamic developments cannot produce only successes at all levels. They also render obsolete certain management practices, which will require adaptation to new ones. The MEW seems to be conscious of the major areas requiring increased effort, sometimes urgently. It is therefore important not so much to dwell on the identification of the related problems, but to design instruments that are capable of solving them. At the level of political priorities, it seems to be of great importance to strengthen the formulation of comprehensive strategic environmental policy objectives, including objectives related to the development of economic sectors. If at all, such strategies exist only with regard to particular aspects of environmental management (such as the water sector), but are neither always complete nor generally accepted. The environmental strategy of 1992 was the last comprehensive strategy to be approved by the Government at large, that of 1994 was the strategy only of the MEW. It is important that such a strategy be endorsed by a broad social consensus, which should pose no substantive problem, since public opinion in this regard has been well prepared. It is also important that such a strategy be fully understood and supported by all staff in the MEW, which suggests that broad in-house discussion should be envisaged and perhaps training courses. The strategy should be fully harmonized with regional development plans, and it should not be difficult to obtain support for its development from UNDP or other funding sources.

Recommendation 1.1:
The Ministry of Environment and Waters should promote, after its completion, the revised national environmental strategy as an absolute priority within the Ministry, the Government at large and the public. Sectoral and regional development plans should be coordinated with it. The strategy should incorporate the international commitments already made, should retain the cooperation of Bulgaria with its neighbours, and should reflect a broad social consensus, i.e. it should be developed with the full participation of the public at large and of economic actors.

A large number of assessments of management practices in Bulgaria appear to have underlined the need for more pronounced horizontal cooperation between the MEW and other ministries and institutions. It is therefore not necessary to dwell at length on this point, although progress appears to be slow. The most promising starting point for the required attitudinal changes can be seen in the efforts being made in anticipation of the negotiations for EU accession. It can be assumed that the EU integration process will become an even more powerful tool for improved coordination at all administrative levels, as it gains momentum. However, additional measures, if successful, would also strengthen Bulgaria's position in the process and should be considered. The concept of sustainable development has shown its capacity to integrate a number of sectoral initiatives with environmental management. A National Commission on Sustainable Development was established in 1999, pursuant to the law on regional development but although the MEW is to chair the commission, it has not yet met. The activities of the "Capacity 21 Task Force" that was established after the Rio Summit with UNDP support could perhaps be integrated into the work of the Commission. The Commission could probably also make use of the Project Management Unit that was established in the Ministry of Regional Development and Public Works with UNDP funding and should, among

other tasks, help to integrate the various initiatives under way for the development of local agendas 21.

Recommendation 1.2:
The National Commission on Sustainable Development should be convened without delay. The Commission should have a broad membership from national, regional and local administrations, as well as from industry and other partners of the NGO community. It should not restrict itself to dealing only with issues that are relevant to the integration of Bulgaria into the European Union, but should also concentrate on designing a strategy for the consistent and integrated development of sustainable sectoral activities.

The formulation of widely accepted social, economic and environmental objectives is certainly a substantial asset in the transition process, but realistic implementation and enforcement plans have to complement them, if unpleasant surprises are to be avoided. It seems that, in general, realistic policies can be more easily achieved with regard to measures that concern the different levels of public environmental management, but many of the required measures primarily affect industrial enterprises. In such cases involving environmental management, contact with the business community is essential. It should have two purposes. On the one hand, the emerging private sector, in the early phases of the EU integration process, is clearly in need of a long-term perspective for its future activities in Europe. On the other, environmental managers would have to develop flexibility of judgement to decide what could or could not be asked of particular companies at a particular time, so that their preparatory efforts for European integration could follow an acceptable time schedule.

The acquisition of such realism in both the business sector and environmental management is a very complex process and cannot be achieved overnight. It is possible that the introduction of cleaner technologies could provide a theme around which a realistic attitude could most easily develop, if it is approached in an appropriate manner. It would be essential to conceive an activity that would unite the private business sector with the MEW. The activity should not only focus on the demonstration of projects that are economically viable and environmentally sustainable, it should also embrace research into enforcement of and compliance with advanced environmental management schemes in accordance with EU practices. Such research should consist of applied investigations into the implications of EU practices in the different industrial sectors. The investigations would benefit from experiences obtained in EU countries or other accession candidates. It is likely that the explicit development of a policy for the introduction of cleaner technologies, as well as the creation of a cleaner technology centre or centres would advance these objectives. Cleaner technology centres would best be jointly financed between the business community and the government and need not wait for the formulation of a specific policy for the introduction of cleaner technologies before being initiated.

Recommendation 1.3:
"Cleaner Production Centres" should be envisaged as undertakings in which the Government and the private business community cooperate, also financing them jointly. Research into the technological adaptation of sectoral industrial production to European practices and promotion of cleaner production in different economic sectors, including demonstration and training programmes, should be considered urgent tasks, which would also be pursued by the "Cleaner Production Centres".

Horizontal cooperation between ministries develops only slowly. Cooperation between the MEW and the Ministry of Health is perhaps the most important of a number of examples. As, in recent years, the readiness to cooperate seems to have grown, more decisive moves would not only be

advantageous, but appear also to be possible. The ongoing revision of the NEHAP provides an opportunity to reconsider cooperation between the two ministries at high level. It might be possible to prepare a decision by the Council of Ministers that would establish an integrated environmental health management system between the ministries, while assigning primary responsibility to one of them. The first product of such cooperation could perhaps be a joint development of those parts of the NEHAP that require joint implementation. The problem of ensuring the flow of monitoring information from the MEW to the Ministry of Health requires an urgent practical solution as the Ministry requires such information for the pursuit of its mandatory functions. It would be a pity, if the advantages of an integrated monitoring system were to be lost, because the problem would remain unresolved. It seems that the envisaged regulation in this area points in the right direction, but practical solutions perhaps need to be found before its adoption. A lasting solution should also clearly specify the integrated monitoring system's source of funding.

Recommendation 1.4:
Regular meetings at an appropriate level should be held between the Ministry of Environment and Waters and the Ministry of Health. They should enable a coordinated implementation of the NEAP and NEHAP, and ensure the flow of environmental monitoring data for the needs of the Ministry of Health.

Chapter 2

ENVIRONMENTAL CONDITIONS AND MANAGEMENT OF POLLUTION AND NATURAL RESOURCES

2.1   Air management

Emissions

Table 2.1:   Emissions of dangerous substances in the ambient air in 1995-1998, and forecast until 2010

	1995	1996	1997	1998	2000	2005	2010
SO$_x$ (as SO$_2$) 10^3 *tonnes/year*	1,476	1,420	1,365	1,251	1,226	890	856
NO$_x$ (as NO$_2$) 10^3 *tonnes/year*	266	259	225	223	280	270	266
NH$_3$ 10^3 *tonnes/year*	99	83	77	66	109	113	108
NMVOCs 10^3 *tonnes/year*	173	147	120	132	185	194	185
CO 10^3 *tonnes/year*	846	613	515	650	820	800	750
CH$_4$ 10^3 *tonnes/year*	506	495	533	553	451	420	420
CO$_2$ *million tonnes/year*	63.1	62.3	59.2	55.1	68	88	101
Lead (Pb) *tonnes*	297.49	278.81	231.24	250.78	347.00	170.90	176.70
Cadmium (Cd) *tonnes*	12.82	14.33	14.23	14.87	12.20	12.50	11.90
Mercury (Hg) *tonnes*	6.88	4.70	4.31	4.69	6.60	6.50	5.80
Dioxins and Furans *Teq/year*	456.00	340.94	309.58	288.43	453.10	433.30	425.00
Hexachlorobenzene (HCB) *kg*	79	87	47	76	84	87	109
Dust (TSP) 10^3 *tonnes/year*	270.0	305.6	265.1	233.2	-	-	-
Polyaromatic hydrocarbons (PAHs) *tonnes/year*	521.43	487.51	419.30	434.02	542.00	574.00	621.00
Pentachlorophenol (PCP) *kg*	10.72	10.61	7.54	9.07	-	-	-
Polychlorinated biphenils (PCBs) *kg*	382.19	261.73	226.99	252.80	-	-	-

Source: Ministry of Environment and Water, Statistical Yearbook, 1998.
Notes:
CO$_2$ emissions for 1995, 1996, 1997 and 1998 are calculated according to IPPC 1996 guidelines;
CO$_2$ emissions for 2000, 2005 and 2010 are baseline scenarios.
Teq: grams toxic equivalents per year (as defined by NATO/CCMS International Toxic Equivalent Scheme).

CO$_2$ The data in Table 2.1 concern the basic compounds that determine ambient air quality (sulphur dioxide, nitrogen dioxide, dust, carbon monoxide) as well as some specific pollutants (lead, mercury, cadmium, dioxins, furans and polyaromatic hydrocarbons).

- The energy industry is a major source of sulphur dioxide (85 per cent), nitrogen dioxide (30 per cent) and dusts (45 per cent).
- The largest anthropogenic sources of volatile organic compounds (VOCs) are road vehicles,

especially petrol-fuelled vehicles (40 per cent), and industry (about 35 per cent). 38 per cent of the nitrogen oxides are due to road transport.

- 71 per cent of methane emissions originate from the extraction and production of fossil fuels. The other significant source of methane is the transport of gas.
- Agriculture is the primary source of ammonia: 50 per cent of the country's total. Another 26 per cent come from the production of nitrogen fertilizers.

- The burning of coal in thermal power plants and the non-ferrous and ferrous metallurgy are the main sources of mercury. The thermal power plants discharge 35.9 per cent of the country's total.
- Almost one third of cadmium emissions are due to the burning of liquid fuels in small combustion facilities at local heating stations.
- Industry and road transport are the main sources of lead pollution.
- The burning of fuels in the domestic sector causes nearly 70 per cent of the emissions of polyaromatic hydrocarbons.
- Combustion processes are the main source of dioxins and furans. Thermal power plants discharge about 40 per cent of the country's total.

Emissions from transport deserve particular attention. The National Environmental Protection Strategy defines the decrease of air pollution from mobile sources as a priority. The total annual emissions from the transport sector [for the different pollutants] are calculated on the basis of statistical fuel consumption data. The significant increase in 1998 emissions compared to 1997 is due to the increase in fuel consumption within the transport sector [for example the consumption of petrol during 1998 is 798 867 tonnes, i.e. 199 944 tonnes higher than in 1997]. In most cases the hot spots are the big cities like Sofia, Burgas, Plovdiv, Rousse, Pernik and others. Vehicle traffic is the major pollution source within these areas.

Table 2.2: Emissions of the main pollutants from transport , 1995-1998

1 000 tonnes

	1995	1996	1997	1998
Total	576.3	510.1	318.7	441.1
SO$_x$	24.1	25.4	23.3	31.4
NMVOC	76.0	64.7	43.0	55.5
NO$_x$	110.0	108.4	83.2	94.2
CO	366.2	311.6	169.2	205.2
Lead *(tonnes)*	153.3	135.9	86.3	109.3

Source: Ministry of Environment and Water.

Other typical ambient air pollutants mostly emitted from the road transport sector are lead aerosols, whose emissions are mainly due to the still prevailing use of leaded petrol. Lead emissions from road transport in 1998 amounted to 109.25 tonnes, or 43.6 per cent of total annual road transport emissions . The increase of 23 tonnes in

comparison with 1997 as already mentioned above is explained by the increased annual consumption of leaded petrol during 1998 (See Table 2.2).

Ambient air quality and main polluted regions

The air quality can be characterized as follows:

Dust. Concentrations are traditionally high throughout the country. The highest average annual concentrations in the country for the past few years, including 1997, have been registered in Pleven, Pernik, St. Zagora, Sofia, Plovdiv, Dimitrovgrad, Rousse, Pirdop (1.2 to 2 times the maximum admissible limit).

Sulphur dioxide. The stabilizing trend in the annual sulphur dioxide concentration close to, but still above, the maximum admissible limit, which started 3-4 years ago, continues. Sulphur dioxide air quality problems prevail in most of the residential areas of Devnia, Plovdiv, Varna, Elisejna, Pernik, Kurdjali, Pirdop (1.2 to 3.5 times the maximum admissible limit - annual average).

Nitrogen dioxide. The highest concentrations of nitrogen dioxide have been measured at busy road junctions in Sofia and Plovdiv, and at stations monitoring industry's impact on air quality in populated areas (Dimitrovgrad and Botunetz). Nitrogen dioxide concentrations caused by vehicles in Sofia, Varna, Plovdiv, Rousse and other cities continue to increase.

Lead aerosols. The annual concentrations of lead aerosols for the country as a whole continue to decrease. The percentage of days with concentrations above the maximum admissible limit (daily average) in Kurdjali fell to 12 per cent in 1997. An exception is the town of Pernik, where the annual concentration has increased by 75 per cent.

Hydrogen sulphide. The highest concentrations are registered in Sofia, Nikopol, Pirdop and Zlatitza, Silistra, Bourgas. Measured concentrations continue to decrease in Pirdop and Zlatitza. In 1998, the maximum admissible limits (annual average) were exceeded in Pirdop and Zlatitza (3 times), in Nikopol (2 times), and in Sofia (3 times).

Ammonia. Air-quality monitoring stations have been set up in settlements with environmental problems related to ammonia-emitting production processes. This is the case in Dimitrovgrad,

Bourgas, Kameno, Nikopol and Vratza. Exceedances of the maximum admissible limit (annual average) vary from a factor of 1 for Dimitrovgrad to a factor of 5 for Nikopol.

Cadmium. Concentrations exceeding the allowed annual limits have been measured in four settlements where cadmium is regularly monitored: Assenovgrad, Kuklen, D. Voden and Plovdiv. The percentage of days in 1997 with concentrations above the maximum admissible limit (daily average) were in Assenovgrad 42 per cent, in D.

Voden 40 per cent, in Kuklen 29 per cent and in Plovdiv (station «Block Gigant») 25 per cent.

The specific objectives derive from the national priorities and the obligations under the global and regional conventions and their protocols that Bulgaria has signed or ratified. They have been set up according to the Convention on Long-range Transboundary Air Pollution and its protocols, the United Nations Framework Convention on Climate Change and its Kyoto Protocol, and the Vienna Convention and the Montreal Protocol. They are summarized in Table 2.3 (a, b, c, d, e)

Basic objectives for reducing air pollution

Table 2.3:   Specific objectives of Bulgaria to reduce air emission levels

	Base year			Target years							Change in % /
	1980	1987	1988	1990	2000	2005	2010	2015	2020	2030	1990
Sulphur dioxide, nitrogen dioxide, VOC and ammonia *(thousand tonnes)* a/											
SO$_2$	2,050	-	-	2,008	1,226	890	856				-57
NO$_x$	-	416	-	361	280	270	266				-26
VOC	-	-	309	217	185	194	185				-15
Ammonia	-	-	-	144	109	113	108				-23
Heavy metals *(tonnes)*											
Lead				436.8	347	170.9	176.7				-60
Cadmium				28.2	12.2	12.5	11.9				-58
Mercury				13.2	6.6	6.5	5.8				-56
Persistent organic pollutants											
Polyaromatic Hydrocarbons *(tonnes)*				677	542	574	621				-8
Dioxins/Furans *(grams)*				554.2	453.1	433.3	425				-23
Hexachlorobenzole *(kilograms)*				544	84	87	109				-80
Emissions of greenhouse gases /Targets under the Kyoto Protocol *(tonnes CO$_2$ equivalent)*											
CO$_2$				96,878	61,741	69,965	72,501	79,060	73,462		
CH$_4$				29,667	19,509	2,755	29,232	30,786	33,243		
N$_2$O				9,548	10,850	12,400	13,020	14,880	14,570		
Total				136,093	92,100	110,316	114,753	124,726	121,275		
Production/use of hydrochlorofluorocarbons (HCFCs)											
				Reduction in % of the baseline level							
HCFCs b/		*1989 base level*			..	..	-100				
Methyl bromide		*1991 base level*		Freeze c/	-25 d/	-50 e/	-70 f/	-100 g/			

Source: Ministry of Environment and Water.

Notes:
a/ According to the new Protocol to Abate Acidification, Eutrophication and Ground-level Ozone to the Convention on Long-range Transboundary Air Pollution (1999).
b/ HCFCs 131, 132, 133, 141, 142, 151, 221, 222, 223, 224, 225, 226, 231, 232, 233, 234, 235, 241, 242, 243, 244, 251, 252, 253, 261, 262, 271.
c/ 1995.
d/ 1999.
e/ 2001.

In addition, the deadline for phasing out leaded petrol has been set at 31 December 2003. To meet this goal, a number of measures will be implemented at different stages; all of them included in a National Programme, adopted by the Government in 1998. The Programme includes legislative, institutional and investment measures.

The objective for ambient air quality is to reach in ambient air the limits for the harmful substances sulphur oxides, airborne particles (PM_{10} and $PM_{2.5}$) and lead, as well as the limits for health and plant protection for ozone by 2006. For nitrogen oxides the objectives would be gradually met in 2005 and 2010. (See section 1.2, Chapter 1 and Chapter 4)

Economic instruments

The 1993 regulation fixing the level of charges was amended in 1999. Pollution charges apply to a series of air pollutants, product charges are levied on fuels and a battery of financial schemes is employed to stimulate cleaner technologies.

2.2   Water management

Situation during 1996-1998

Water quality. There is no evidence of any improvement in river quality since 1996, even though the pressure from industry and agriculture on water and water sources has continued to decline. Pollution treatment capacity has not significantly expanded, nor has the operation of existing facilities improved. In addition to the financial problems that monitoring faces, the raw data are not transformed into information describing the water quality throughout the territory, so it is difficult to give a precise picture of the overall situation.

Water use. The total amount of fresh water abstracted during the 1996-1998 period was 3.1-3.5 billion cubic metres a year (Table 2.4), 73 per cent to 76 per cent surface water and 24 per cent to 27 per cent groundwater. While the consumption of surface water was rather stable, there was a drop in the use of groundwater, because less groundwater was used for irrigation and by industry. The sharp decrease in industrial use is noticeable both in the water quantities delivered by the public supply system and in the private uptakes (Table 2.4 and 2.5).

Table 2.4: Water abstraction, 1996-1998

Million m³

	1996	1997	1998
Total	**3,457**	**3,096**	**3,476**
Surface waters	2,531	2,251	2,635
Groundwater	918	838	835
Other waters	8	7	6
Abstracted by:			
Public water system	2,191	1,967	2,407
Self abstraction by enterprises *	1,265	1,129	1,069

Source: National Statistical Institute.

* Enterprises which uptake over 36 000 m³/year.

Table 2.5: Public water supply, 1996-1998

Million m³

	1996	1997	1998
Total	**1,292**	**978**	**897**
Domestic use	677	422	302 *
Agriculture	257	207	197
Industry	357	349	268 **
Others	-	-	130 *
Losses in the distribution system			
as % of abstracted water	*41*	*50*	*58*

Source: National Statistical Institute.

* In 1998, water for domestic use has been splitted into "Domestic use" and "Others".

** Of which: chemicals production (141 million m³), ferro metallurgy (65 million m³) and food industry (59 million m³).

Abstraction and use of groundwater. Groundwater is used mainly in households and to a lesser extent for industrial and irrigation purposes. Figure 2.1 shows the abstraction of groundwater by type of source. The most common source is wells (51 per cent). The type of source is very much determined by the hydro-geological characteristics of each individual area. For instance, the Sliven district uses very little spring water (no more than 0.27 per cent), while springs are by far the largest source in the Pernik district (94 per cent). In the district of Silistra, all extracted groundwater comes from wells.

Waste water and its treatment. The total quantity of waste water discharged from industry and public sewage systems during the 1996-1998 period was about 1.1 billion m³ a year, as shown in Table 2.6.

While the quantities of waste water removed in 1996 and 1997 were almost the same, the quantity in 1998 was substantially lower, mainly due to a reduction in the quantity of industrial waste water. The quantities treated are stable. In 1998, 58 per cent of waste water was subject to some kind of treatment. Industry, agriculture and forestry generated 523 million cubic metres of waste water in 1998, some of it reused and 473 million discharged. This is 12 per cent less than in 1997. 214 billion cubic metres, or 45 per cent, of industrial waste water remain untreated. 55 per cent of this water flows into surface waters, about 2 per cent into the sea and the underground, and 43 per cent is discharged into the public sewage systems. The chemical, steel and oil-refining industries release 328 billion cubic metres of waste water,

Figure 2.1: Abstraction of groundwater by sources, 1998

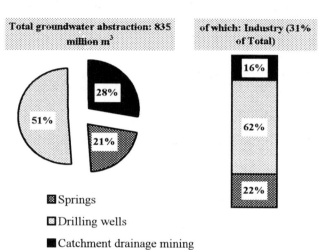

■ Springs
□ Drilling wells
■ Catchment drainage mining

Source: National Statistical Institute.

Table 2.6: Industrial waste-water discharges and treatment, 1996-1998

Million m³

	Total	of which: treated	Discharged directly by industry into surface water bodies		Discharged to public sewerage	
			Total	of which: treated	Total	of which: treated
1996	1,160	724	488	319	672	405
1997	1,152	702	407	269	746	433
1998	1,019	647	349	225	670	422

Source: National Statistical Institute.

The share of waste water generated by the economic sectors in 1998 was:

- 88.4 per cent by industry, including
  - 10 per cent by mining
  - 67.9 per cent by the processing industry (mostly chemicals, oil refining and steel industry)
  - 9.2 per cent by the production and re-distribution of energy;
  - 1.2 per cent by the construction industry
- 3.1 per cent by agriculture and forestry;
- 8.0 per cent by other sectors and activities.

65 per cent of which is treated. Most of the waste water from chemicals and oil refining industries is discharged into the sea, while the steel industry ranks first in releasing waste water into surface reservoirs. The enterprises in these sectors pollute water with organic substances, mineral salts, toxic heavy metals, cyanides, oil products, etc.

70 per cent of the population is connected to a sewage system. 104 towns in Bulgaria have a population above 10 000, 28 above 50 000. There are 51 municipal waste-water treatment plants, 14 of them offering only mechanical treatment and 37 using biological treatment. These plants serve 51 cities, or 35.7 per cent of the country's total population. Data about the treatment of waste water collected by public sewage systems in 1998 are shown in Figure 2.2.

In 1998, about 2 million tonnes of dry solids were produced as sludge in the waste-water treatment units (See Figure 2.3). Most of this sludge is just landfilled without other treatment. Sometimes sludge is used in the rehabilitation of mines. Very little is used in agriculture as fertilizer.

New waste-water treatment plants were commissioned during the 1996-1999 period in Kavarna, Pomorie, Strazhitsa (mechanical stage), Tervel and General Toshevo. Other projects continue, as explained in Chapter 3.

Management strategy and instruments

In 1997, a Strategy for Integrated Water Management was drafted for the years 1997-2002.

Figure 2.2: Waste-water treatment by public sewage systems, 1998

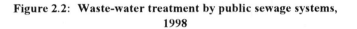

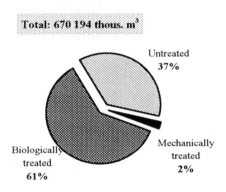

Source: National Statistical Institute.

Figure 2.3: Sludge production in waste-water treatment, 1998

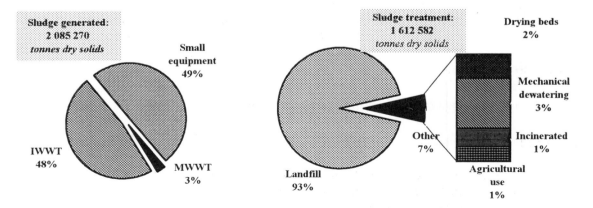

Source: National Statistical Institute.

It is an excellent institutional project, but the available financial and technical capacities are not consistent with the proposed schedule. The most important step forward has been the adoption of the Water Act of July 1999 (see Chapter 1). The organization of water management by river basin is foreseen and appropriately designed, but the difficulties, training, user and public support, cost and time for this process are underestimated and there is no precise plan of action. The situation is assessed in detail in Chapter 5.

A licensing system was established for the use of water and water facilities based on the new 1999 Water Act. The system encompasses:

- Licences for the use of surface waters and groundwaters, including mineral waters that are not subject to concessions
- Licences for the use of water facilities, including:
  - the construction, reconstruction or modernization of systems and equipment for regulating outflows, drinking water infrastructure, infrastructure crossing water such as aqueducts, bridges, power transmission networks, exploration and production of groundwaters, protection against flooding, dredging, production of sand and gravel, water sports and recreation
  - industrial fishing, aquaculture of fish and other biological resources
- Licences issued for other specific purposes that will have an impact on the natural state of the water source, including on river sections and draining reservoirs
- Licences for the discharge of waste water.

The new system for monitoring the chemical quality of surface water complies with EU standards, but the necessary data analysis, aggregation and presentation are not yet available for useful water quality assessment (See Chapter 5).

According to the 1999 Water Act, general water use and the use of water and water facilities for personal needs are free of charge. Any landowner is entitled to freely use the surface and ground waters on his plot in a quantity that may not exceed 0.2 litres per second and 10 cubic metres per 24-hour period, as well as surface waters outside his plot for the purpose of irrigating a plot of land not exceeding 20 ares with no more than 300 cubic metres of water per 10 ares a month.

A natural resource use fee was introduced for the use of water and water facilities for business purposes. It guarantees equal legal terms for the businesses whether operated by natural or legal persons. This fee is payable by the holder of the licence for the quantities of water removed from the source where consumption is measured.

Regarding public supply, customers pay for drinking water and sewerage (See Chapter 5). Every family was compelled to install a water meter before 2000 at its own expense. Water supply companies charge only for the quantities of water actually delivered to consumers. After 2004, if general water losses sustained by water supply companies exceed 25 per cent (they average 52 per cent at present), these will not be incorporated in the price of the water supply service.

Hefty fines enforce the law. The unlicensed use of water, or use that does not comply with the terms and conditions of the licence or contract; use of water facilities and equipment or the construction of such facilities and equipment without a licence or in violation of the terms and conditions of the licence or contract; water pollution, destruction of riverbeds or shores; allowing waste waters to reach water facilities or canals leading to violations of emissions or intake norms and standards; nondisclosure of information on incidents involving water facilities; damage or destruction of stations that are part of the national monitoring network; the commercial sale of mineral water without the necessary certificates, etc., are all fined.

The penal provisions were developed in compliance with the water legislation of the European Union. The sanctions are commensurate with the damage caused, with the liability insurance and with the mechanisms for correcting the damage. Fines are in amounts ranging from 150 to 25,000 leva, while repeat violators are fined from 1000 to 50,000 leva.

Responsible institutions

Management of water at national level is the exclusive prerogative of the Council of Ministers, exercised since 1997 through the Ministry of Environment and Waters. The Ministry of Regional Development and Public Works implements the national policy in public works, in particular the development of water supply and sewerage systems (see Chapter 1).

The Water Act sets up new territorial management of water by catchment area. Management at basin level will be carried out by 4 basin directorates, assisted by basin boards made up of representatives of the government, the local administration, water users and environmental organizations operating in the area of the basin, as well as representatives of water research organizations. This scheme is only partially implemented and according to the 1997 Strategy for the Integrated Management of Water is prepared jointly by the MEW and MRDPW.

Municipalities manage water facilities that are municipal property. Among their responsibilities are the building, maintenance and proper use of waste-water treatment plants, the operation of water supply systems and sewerage that are the property of the municipality, and the construction and registration of wells for individual use of groundwaters on the territory of the municipality.

The Ministry of Health monitors the quality of drinking water and medicinal water, including bottled water. Hydrological monitoring of water is the task of the National Institute of Hydrology, and physico-chemical monitoring that of the Executive Environmental Agency.

2.3   Waste management and soil rehabilitation

Waste generation

According to present waste statistics, the amount of waste generated in 1998 was about 35 million tonnes, mainly industrial waste. Mining and quarrying waste represented 188 million tonnes in the same year, an amount which has been rather stable in recent years. Table 2.7 shows the distribution of the waste generated by type during the period.

Table 2.7: Generation of waste, 1997-1998

Type of waste	Units	1997	1998
Municipal	10^3 tonnes	3,628	3,197
Construction	10^3 m^3	805	1,023
Mining and quarrying	10^3 tonnes	187,083	187,964
Other industrial	10^3 tonnes	43,586	30,473
Hazardous	10^3 tonnes	1,100	548

Source: National Statistical Institute.

Municipal waste. In 1995-1997, between 450 and 500 kg of municipal waste was generated on average per person a year. The 3.6 million tonnes of municipal waste registered in 1997 were generated in 1,126 settlements with organized

waste collection and transport, serving 77 per cent of the country's population.

Disposal is the only municipal waste treatment at present. There were 622 landfills for controlled waste disposal in 1998, and 99 per cent of the collected waste accumulated there. With a few exceptions, these landfills do not comply with the new requirements. According to the data supplied by the municipal administrations, almost 27 per cent of the existing landfills are under their control. They represent 54 per cent of the area covered by landfills.

Construction waste. More than 80 per cent of construction waste are generated in the country's big cities. About 300,000 m^3 of the construction waste is collected into specialized landfills. A quarter are used in road construction and the recultivation of soils. There are cases of construction waste being discharged into landfills for municipal waste, but this practice is now rare.

Industrial waste. 43.5 million tonnes of industrial waste was generated in 1997, 30.5 in 1998. In relative terms, mining and ore-processing industries generate the most industrial waste. Part of their waste is hazardous. Thermal power plants and chemical industries are the next biggest industrial waste generators.

Table 2.8: Generation and disposal of industrial * waste, 1997-1998

	Thousand tonnes	
	1997	**1998**
Total generated	**43,586**	**30,473**
Organic	1,418	1,129
Inorganic	42,168	29,344
Landfill**	**43,024**	**30,142**
Organic	1,171	904
Inorganic	41,853	29,238

Source: Executive Environmental Agency.

*   Excludes mining and quarrying waste.

** Public or owned by the enterprises.

The mining and ore-processing enterprises which are declared bankrupt or in receivership are facing serious problems with their tailings ponds. The total area damaged by such enterprises exceeds 1670 hectares, 510 ha of which are old tailings ponds. More than 270 million tonnes of hazardous waste is deposited in the latter, resulting from the processing of copper-pyrite and lead-zinc ores.

Disposal in landfills is the most common industrial-waste treatment method. Over 99 per cent of the waste is deposited in landfills owned by the enterprises themselves and the rest is deposited in the urban landfills together with municipal waste. The waste from the food industry is often (61 per cent) reused in agriculture as food for livestock and as fertilizer. The rest is deposited in urban landfills together with municipal waste.

The enterprises report that ferrous and non-ferrous metal (98 per cent), paper (89 per cent) and glass (62 per cent) waste are largely recycled. Depending on the way activities are organized within the respective industrial units, the collected waste is directly transferred to recycling companies or to licensed trading companies.

Hazardous waste. The average annual amount of hazardous waste generated in Bulgaria in recent years is about 1.1 million tonnes, 40 per cent of which are of the 11 most common types (pesticides, waste oils, sludge from industrial waste water, hospital waste, etc.) Data on the hazardous waste generated do not include waste generated by primary processing of non-ferrous metal ores, which are shown together with the waste generated by mining and ore-processing enterprises. The information available represents mainly waste quantities. The absence of a national laboratory system for hazardous waste does not allow more precise identification by material and control of the waste.

Over 500 enterprises generate less than 1,000 tonnes/year, about 40 enterprises generate between 1,000 and 10,000 tonnes/year and 14 enterprises generate over 10,000 tonnes/year. About 30 enterprises generate more than 90 per cent of the hazardous waste in Bulgaria. These same enterprises also tend to treat their own waste.

The main method for hazardous waste treatment is landfilling (77 per cent) on-site. These landfills have exhausted their capacity and do not comply with the requirements of the modern national legislation, which is already harmonized with the relevant European Union directives. There are several waste incinerators but they can barely cope with the waste of the companies for which they were constructed. Incinerators of hospital wastes have been built in some of the big cities and former district centres. However, they rarely comply with modern requirements for installations of this type and they do not treat waste from all clinics in their regions.

The problem of obsolete pesticides has been temporarily solved. A small part was exported to be burnt in the Netherlands. Another part has been safely stored in containers cased in concrete. The remaining will be deposited in the future landfills for hazardous waste disposal.

Waste generated from uranium-ore mining and processing. 40 mines and two hydro-metallurgical works generate (or generated) uranium containing waste in Bulgaria. More than 20 million tonnes of waste were deposited in 3 tailing ponds and about 300 waste banks. Uranium mines discharge more than 1,000 litres of contaminated water a second. Rock waste banks have radioactivity levels 2 to 100 times higher than the background values.

The main pollution features of the water discharged from the closed uranium sites are:

- uranium concentration: 0.1 - 15 mg/l, depending on season flow rate of the diluting water
- radium 226 concentration: 0.08 - 1.5 Bq/l
- pH value: 3 - 8
- sulphate concentration: up to 19 500 mg/l.

The regions posing the biggest risk to human health from a radiological point of view are Buhovo, Yana, Seslavtsi, Eleshnitsa and Sliven. In the past, mining and hydro-metallurgical processing was very high there. Rehabilitation activities were undertaken with priority for these regions.

Soil pollution

The main problems are deposition of air pollutants from metallurgical plants, soil acidification due to over-fertilization and soil erosion. According to data of 1996, 393 hectares have been damaged by mining, quarrying or other similar works. Coal mining is chiefly responsible (almost 90 per cent). 49 ha have been restored, which is only 12 per cent of the affected lands. There is an increase in damaged areas.

Pollution by heavy metals. In 1996, some more precise investigations into soil pollution estimated the surface polluted by heavy metals and metalloids at 43000 ha, of which 7700 heavily polluted and potentially dangerous for human health. Four hot spots are located around big ferrous and non-ferrous metallurgical sites, power plants and oil-processing plants: in particular, a non-ferrous metallurgical factory in Plovdiv, a metallurgical establishment in Kremikovtzi near Sofia, a copper refinery in Pirdop and a metallurgical works in Eliseyna. The heavy metal content of soil in these places is increasing more slowly since industrial activity eased off. Other soil pollution by heavy metals has been noticed as a result of phytoprotective treatment in orchards and vineyards (Cu, Mo and Zn), the emissions of vehicles along roads (Pb), and irrigation practices using mine water (Pb, Zn, As, Cd).

The certificates given to farmers at land restitution included information on its pollution characteristics and specified what kind of agriculture was authorized on the plots. They even provided for compensation for the restrictions. However, no compensation has been received so far. Farmers were encouraged to grow technical crops, such as cotton or flax, for instance in the Plovdiv region.

A few pilot projects have been launched recently. In the region ofPirdop and Zlatiza, the MAF finances a project aiming at blocking heavy metals in-situ, so that they will not migrate down to the aquifers, nor be incorporated into plants. The method is based on the treatment of soil with lime. Other pilot projects aimed at accumulating heavy metals in plants (phytoaccumulation) are carried out in Plovdiv andChremikovci. The Institute for Genetical Engineering in Kostinbrod is developing a testing programme for high accumulating plants.

Fertilizers and pesticides. Another problem was the widespread acidification of soils by an overuse of fertilizers before 1990. The use of artificial fertilizers has drastically dropped since 1995, i.e. minus 25 per cent over the past three years, as the use of organic fertilizers (manure) has increased. This results in a natural restoration of soils. The situation is similar regarding pollution with pesticides, which are now used far less. However, the 1998 State of the Environment report points out that DDT derivatives were found in many sites in alarmingly high concentrations. This requires urgent investigations in the whole country. In particular, the storage and possible current use of derivatives of the DDT family should be checked. PAHs (polyaromatic hydrocarbons) have been found in a few places close to industrial sites. However, none of the samples has reached the background level for cultivated lands (German background values used as reference). In most cases PCB levels in the investigated regions were below the detection levels. In general, the monitoring of soils and groundwater shows that there is at present no pollution by pesticides. Spring waters are also of good quality.

Waste management strategies and measures

A National Waste Management Programme was approved by the Council of Ministers in March 1999. The National Programme comprises an Action Plan and an Investment Programme for the period up to 2002. It sets out specific institutional and investment measures that are to be initiated in the next four years. The measures laid down in the Programme have deadlines and designated implementing bodies. It specifies both the necessary funding and the funding source. 678 billion leva (i.e. about US$ 340 million) are needed to implement the programme from 1999 to 2002. A large amount will be provided by domestic sources (56 per cent).

To set priorities, the criteria applied were: risk to human health; impact on vulnerable ecosystems; national or regional significance of the project; compliance with the new legislation; fulfilment of Bulgaria's international obligations; the degree of project maturity for implementation; and financial factors. Based on these criteria, the priorities focus on:

- waste in the closed uranium mining sites
- hazardous waste generated by industry
- municipal waste.

The Programme foresees prevention and reduction of wastes; reuse and recycling; improving waste collection and transport; safe waste disposal; cleaning up pollution; improvement of the regulatory framework; public awareness raising and improving monitoring and information. On their basis, investment projects were decided:

- Cleaning-up of 60 uranium mining and processing sites
- Establishment of a regional centre for hazardous waste treatment
- Construction of 4 landfills for hazardous waste
- Building and reconstruction of 37 regional landfills for municipal waste
- Cleaning up contamination caused by selected large industrial enterprises
- Implementation of the Programme for Sanitation of Hazardous Waste, deposited by flotation of non-ferrous ore in enterprises in liquidation (6 tailings ponds)
- Construction of incinerators for hospital waste
- Construction of facilities for the treatment of municipal waste-water treatment sludge and their possible use in agriculture

- Establishing of a centre for the dismantling of old vehicles
- Construction of an installation for composting municipal waste
- Modernization of the existing and construction of new facilities for waste recycling (waste oils, PET bottles, batteries, etc.)
- Renovation of special containers and equipment for waste collection and transport.

Three regional landfills have already been constructed with the financial assistance of the European Union's Instrument for Structural Policies for Pre-Accession (ISPA covering 75 per cent of total investment cost).

In parallel to the National Waste Management Programme, the roughly 270 municipalities of the country have been requested to prepare their own municipal waste management programme within a year from the promulgation of the National Programme. By spring 2000, about 75 per cent of them had done so. Similarly, about 1300 industrial companies also have to draw up their programme. All programmes are submitted to the regional inspectorates of the MEW for approval.

The municipalities state in their programmes their current situation and problems, their approach for the future and their action plan to reach their objectives. They evaluate their financial needs and propose a financing scheme. Only actions envisaged in their programmes will be eligible for financial assistance from the State. Assistance is available for equipment for the collection, handling and transport of waste but not for the improvement of municipal landfills. In addition, the law (Regulation 13, art. 45) obliges the municipalities to bring their landfills step by step in compliance with sanitary requirements when they use them. This is a way of encouraging municipalities to turn to new regional landfills and to contract out the collection, handling and transport of their waste to concessionaires. The financial assistance given by the State is through loans, and municipalities are likely to be tempted to realize economies of scale through joint solutions.

It is likely that the result of this strategy will be to put municipal waste management in the hands of concessionaires, who will make the necessary investments and even pay higher transport costs to the more distant regional landfills. The drawback is a foreseeable important increase in the user fee, which some people will find difficult to afford. Also the time frame to achieve such big

investments seems unrealistically tight, taking into account the overall economic difficulties of the country and the other investments made to improve water management.

The application of the waste management programmes of industrial plants is facilitated by the environmental audits undertaken at the time of privatization (see Chapter 1 for a description).

Soil rehabilitation measures

The Ministry of Environment and Waters has allocated major financial resources to the operation and management of a national system of environmental monitoring for soils and lands. The issue of the quality of soil and land and of contaminated sites now draws the attention of the public and the mass media. Cooperation on related projects is developing with other countries. As these problems can have an impact on human health, a higher priority will be given to solving them.

2.4 Nature management

Recent developments and current situation

According to data of 1995-2000, Bulgaria's biota is very rich. It includes about 27000 insects and other invertebrate species, 3550-3783 vascular plants, more than 6500 non-vascular plants and fungi, up to 736 vertebrates (of which 81-94 mammals, 374-383 birds, 33-36 reptiles, 16-17 amphibians, and 207 seawater and freshwater fish). Despite its small territory, Bulgaria is rich in endemic species. About 200 endemic species of the Balkans have been found in Bulgaria: invertebrate non-insects 8.8 per cent, insects 4.3 per cent, plants 5 per cent, freshwater fish 5.7 per cent, amphibians 5.8 per cent, reptiles 11.1 per cent, and mammals 4.3 per cent.

Due to the increasing anthropogenic pressures of the past decades, a few species are extinct. Among them, 27-31 species of vascular plants, 7 invertebrates, 3 fish, 2 reptiles, 3 birds, 2 mammals. Six breeds of indigenous domestic animals have also disappeared. Rare flora and fauna include more than 700 vascular plants, 567 non-insects, more than 1500 insects, 29 fish, 2 reptiles, 78 birds (of which 16 are on the 1993 IUCN list of Globally Threatened Species) and 10 large mammals. During the past three years 327 birds, 389 plants, 473 animals and 1766 trees have been registered as protected species.

In 1998, forests covered 30.2 per cent of the territory. Coniferous trees represented 33 per cent of the total. The forest coverage and coniferous trees are on the increase: in 2005, forest cover will reach 31 per cent of the territory and the coniferous share 49.2 per cent.

Management strategy and instruments

In 1998, Bulgaria's Council of Ministers adopted the Strategy for the Conservation of Biological Diversity, and in 1999 the National Biodiversity Conservation Programme. The Programme contains

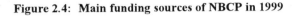

Figure 2.4: Main funding sources of NBCP in 1999

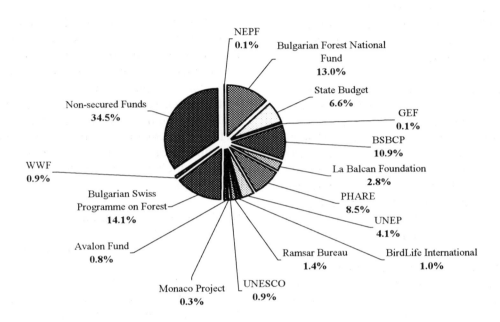

Source: National Conservation Biodiversity Plan.

Figure 2.5: Budgetary sources of planned State funding of NBCP, 2000

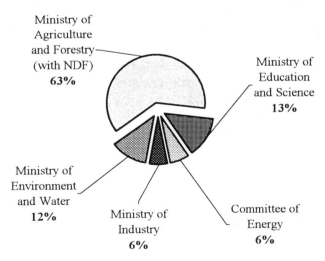

Source: National Conservation Biodiversity Plan.

a number of activities that might be implemented in the period 1999-2003, provided that the MEW determines priorities among these activities.

The National Biodiversity Conservation Programme (NBCP), which was approved by the Council of Ministers in August 1999 and published with financial support of UNDP in February 2000, lists 43 new legal instruments that are expected to be introduced by 2003, including: a biodiversity law (a structure exists), a Black Sea coast law, a mountain areas law, a law on the protection of old plant varieties and agricultural animal breeds, secondary legislation under the Forest Law, a regulation on the sustainable use and maintenance of meadows and pastures, a strategy for the sustainable use of medicinal plants, a strategy for the conservation and management of forest ecosystem biodiversity, a programme for integrated plant protection in forests, etc. It is estimated that the total NBCP cost would be 44,355,000 leva for the five-year period (1999-2003). 23,081,000 leva are secured for 2000.

Action plans for the conservation of species have been implemented, mainly for globally threatened species, such as the Dalmatian pelican, pigmy cormorant, ferruginous duck, white-tailed eagle, imperial eagle, lesser kestrel and corncrake, etc. (by the Bulgarian Society for the Protection of Birds), and for mammals, such as bear, marbled polecat, bats (by the Wilderness Fund and Green Balkans). Several action plans aiming for the sustainable development of forest and/or mountain communities have also been developed with the support of international programmes. They support NGOs and State organizations for actions in the Central Balkan, Rila, Pirin and Rhodope mountain areas.

All forests in Bulgaria are managed and exploited according to the Forest Law, regulations for forest management, and the National Strategy on Forestry and Forest Management of 1996, reinforced by the State Programme on Management and Control of Forest Resources of 1998. The management structure includes the Forestry Committee, 16 Regional Forestry Boards and 164 Forest Estates. All forest territories are State-owned, since nationalization in 1947. The restoration of ownership rights to municipal forestland (57 per cent of the forest prior to 1947) and private forestland (19 per cent before 1947) is expected.

Regarding habitat protection, the trends in protected areas are shown in Figure 7.2. The privatization of land has an important impact on the management of protected areas. As of April 2000, two categories of protected areas (reserves and national parks) are exclusively in State ownership, and four others (nature monuments, maintained reserves, nature parks, protected sites) include other forms of ownership: either exclusive State ownership or State and municipal or private ownership (See table 7.1 in chapter 7). Protected areas have been reclassified and are subject to further extension. This is explained in Chapter 7.

The current financial mechanisms foresee that management activities will be funded by the State budget and external sources, international projects and programmes, the National Environmental Protection Fund, the Bulgarian Forest National Fund, etc. (for details, see Figures 2.4 and 2.5). The NEPF has organized annual competitions for NGOs and provided financing for 50 public environmental projects. Nearly 200 municipal environmental conservation funds are involved in funding at regional levels. In addition to the financial mechanisms, the usual major administrative and regulatory mechanisms (EIA, permits, sanctions, etc.) continue to be applied.

Management responsibilities

The conservation of biological diversity and the sustainable use of natural resources are managed and controlled by several government institutions. The National Nature Protection Service of the MEW is the central authority, together with its regional administrations. The National Centre for Environment and Sustainable Development of the MEW completes the annual Green Book of Bulgaria (i.e. the State of the Environment report), keeps and collects information about hunting, forestry, etc. The National Statistical Institute is involved in collecting information on biodiversity and protected areas. It issues the "Report on protected territories and objects", describing the state of 11 protected areas or objects, i.e. categories of protected areas, protected animal and plant species and protected trees. For details, see Chapter 7.

The Ministry of Agriculture and Forestry and its units are responsible for the conservation of biological diversity and the sustainable use of forest and agricultural resources in large parts of the country. An administrative unit for nature parks – the Protected Areas Department – was created at the Forestry Committee. Other national and international governmental and non-governmental organizations are involved in financing and conserving biological diversity in Bulgaria, providing relevant monitoring, including in protected areas. The Ministry of Regional Development and Public Works oversees the efficient use of land, energy and other resources, as well as sustainable development at regional and municipal levels, including in the coastal zone.

The other major State bodies involved are the regional and municipal councils and the local self-administration authorities, the Ministry of Economy, the Ministry of Education and Science, and theState Agency on Energy and Energy Resources.

NGOs play also an active role in the conservation of species, as well as the formulation of proposals for action. Since its foundation in 1998, the Bulgarian Society for the Protection of Birds, together with the State nature conservation institutions, has taken part in activities to protect globally threatened species. Action plans were developed for the conservation of globally threatened species such as the Dalmatian Pelican, the Pigmy Cormorant, the Ferruginous Duck, the

White-tailed Eagle, the Imperial Eagle, the Lesser Kestrel, the Corncrake, etc. (by the Bulgarian Society for the Protection of Birds), and for some mammals, such as bears, marbled polecats, and bats (by the Wilderness Fund and Green Balkans). Bulgaria is responsible for actions concerning three species in defined sites (the Dalmatian Pelican on Shebrana Lake, the White-headed Duck on Uzungeren Bay, and the Imperial Eagle everywhere, in cooperation with Hungary and Slovakia).

2.5   Management of mineral resources

Major reserves and mining

The mining activities in Bulgaria over recent years, as well as the assessment of remaining reserves in 1999, are shown in Table 2.9.

Management strategy and instruments

Since the adoption of the Underground Resources Act and all required supplementary acts, 60 applications for permits or concessions were in process, and 20 had been signed between March

Table 2.9: Exploitation of mineral resources, 1995-99

	1995	1996	1997	1998	1999	Resources (01.01.1999)
Coal *(Thous. tonnes)*	31,836	32,209	29,310	31,248	25,893	4,657,560
Lignite	27,449	28,130	25,880	27,435	22,696	3,892,510
Brown	4,156	3,965	3,370	3,692	3,074	338,983
Black	205	169	44	105	106	423,967
Anthracite	26	24	16	16	17	2,100
Petrol *(Thous. tonnes)*	29	34	27	32	39	603
Natural gas *(Million m³)*	50	..	41	33	27	2,245
Metal ores *(Thous. tonnes)*	23,488	24,388	24,876	23,441	24,281	1,315,208
Cu - containing	20,853	21,692	21,908	20,726	22,346	823,433
Pb - Zn containing	1,717	1,527	1,420	1,158	604	102,598
Pb - Ag containing	34	42	62	13	..	6,586
Fe - containing	824	1,002	832	895	699	199,202
Mn - containing	19	44	47	56	..	125,499
Au - containing	40	560	610	593	632	57,890
Industrial mineral resources *(Thous. tonnes)*	4,330	6,576	8,614	4,265	..	4,114,574
Res. for cement production *(Thous. tonnes)*	6,650	5,582	4,019	1,598	..	2,138,314
Rocky materials for decoration *(Thous. m³)*	61	69	191	138	..	286,331
Materials for constructions and ceramic industry *(Thous. m³)*	..	5,055	6,571	3,566	..	1,808,686

Source: Ministry of Environment and Waters.

1999 and April 2000. The management of mineral resources is today entrusted to several governmental institutions, depending on the type of resource, the area concerned or the management aspect. The MEW has large responsibilities in the development of State policies, for instance to encourage investments. The MEW organizes tenders for permits for prospecting or exploration and the conclusion of contracts for most parts of Bulgaria (after approval by the Council of Ministers). The Underground Resources Act stipulates that such strategies and policies should be formulated in view of the sustainable development of the country. The MEW is also the main institution that oversees the information work in this field (i.e. funding of geological research, collection, processing, storage and dissemination of geological information through the Geofund, organization of relevant registers and cadastres and other records, as well as the compilation of national balances of reserves and resources).

The Minister of Industry is responsible for the implementation of actual mining. Concessions for mining are usually given by the Council of Ministers. Municipal councils may give concessions for the production of construction materials up to 10,000 m^3 annually, after agreement by the MEW. The permitting activities of the Ministry of Industry concern metallic and mineral resources, as well as precious and semi-precious stones and certain types of technological wastes, in the continental shelf and the exclusive economic zone of the Black Sea. Analogous responsibilities are entrusted to the Minister for Regional Development and Public Works regarding resources used in construction works, and to the Chairman of the State Agency for Energy and Energy Resources regarding energy resources.

Prospecting and exploration require permits, and the production of mineral resources is subject to concession. Permits are linked to specified types of resources and areas. Their duration is initially three years, but can be extended. The discovery of deposits entitles the holder of the exploration or prospecting permit to a production concession. Production concessions can be given for periods up to 35 years, with a possible extension of up to 15 years. A storage and utilization plan for the waste from production and primary processing is obligatory and has to be approved by the competent ministry and agreed by the MEW. Special reference is made in the Underground Resources Act to the provisions of the Act on Restriction of Harmful Impact of Waste on the Environment.

The normal procedure (i.e. direct nomination of a holder of a prospecting or exploration permit in the case of the discovery of a deposit) for obtaining a permit for prospecting or exploration and concessions for production is through tender. The contract on which prospecting, exploration or production is eventually based includes terms and conditions of inspection of the sites concerned. Termination of prospecting, exploration or production requires the holder of title to repair the inflicted damage to the land in accordance with the applicable legislation on environmental protection and/or other specified provisions.

Furthermore, the Underground Resources Act contains a part dealing with the protection of the underground and the rational use of mineral resources. It specifies conditions for activities and State supervisory functions by the MEW. Rehabilitation of terrains is subject to projects that are to be coordinated with the MEW.

2.6   Conclusions

Air management

Since the first Environmental Performance Review in 1995, the main parameters characterizing air quality have been steadily improving. The reasons are varied: from the relative drop in industrial and energy production to the implementation of modern and optimized monitoring and the enforcement of legal measures adopted in the country.

The economic, social and other problems associated with the transition period make the practical and immediate implementation of the newly adopted norms and standards difficult. Many initiatives suffer from a lack of adequate financial support. This is especially true of the adaptation of the institutional framework that predetermines, for most of the normative acts, the introduction of transitional provisions, shifting to a later date their full application. For instance, it has not been possible to set up a system to warn the public in real time when air emission concentrations overshoot certain limits because of a lack of funding. A better evaluation and analysis of the mechanisms of domestic and international financing for air protection management in the country would certainly be needed.

Water management

While there is no evidence that the situation of

waters in Bulgaria has improved much since the previous EPR, many projects are currently going on that will profoundly modify the managerial structures and infrastructure in water protection. With the implementation of the new legal framework and the introduction of EU directives into water management, modern concepts of water management are introduced. Also the infrastructure in water distribution and waste-water treatment will much improve in the near future as important investments are foreseen. Nevertheless, managing water in a sustainable way will still necessitate a few other actions that are assessed and proposed in Chapter 5.

Waste management and soil rehabilitation

The new waste management programme foresees the necessary infrastructure for a successful management of waste, applying the relevant principles and practices of the EU. However, the acceptance by the local administration and the public, be they citizens or enterprises, is a criterion that should not be underestimated. In particular, because the new waste strategy will necessitate many changes in behaviour and certainly a large financial effort from everyone. Awareness campaigns about the upcoming waste management practices might be able to ensure individual participation and acceptance. NGOs should be actively involved in such campaigns. Discussions about ways to optimize waste management at municipal and regional level should be held to consider opportunities for cost reduction by

developing schemes regrouping several municipalities.

Nature management

Regarding the conservation of biodiversity, the current delays could be overcome if the Ministry of Environment and Waters clearly and promptly formulated the priorities in an action plan. The programme suggests a large number of well-prepared projects, and foreign assistance can be expected for their implementation, once the priorities are clear.

Management of mineral resources

The relatively recent inclusion of mineral resource management into the Ministry of Environment and Waters does not appear to have led to the full integration of the various new functions of the MEW. The opportunities offered by this institutional rearrangement should not be lost. They include the potential for integrating environmental policy objectives into the actual exploitation of mineral resources, as well as the integration of such resource use into the sustainable development of the country. The MEW might have to show that it is willing to take on the corresponding challenge by developing a comprehensive management scheme for all mineral resources, in cooperation with the various institutions that are at present involved in related tasks.

PART II: CURRENT PRIORITIES OF ENVIRONMENTAL POLICY AND MANAGEMENT

Chapter 3

DEVELOPMENT OF SOURCES OF FINANCE FOR ENVIRONMENTAL PROTECTION INVESTMENTS

3.1 Funding sources and their financing instruments

Types of investment funding

In the following, the term 'investment financing' refers to all types of funding assistance to environmental projects, such as:

- direct/capital investment support
- grants, donations and budget subsidies (including exemptions from import taxes, duties or VAT)
- soft loans (interest-free or at below-market interest rates)
- loans at market interest rates and conditions
- equity (participation with share capital)
- issuance of bonds
- indirect investment support (e.g. provision of related services or equipment, etc.)
- technical assistance (project preparation/management, technical assessments, EIA, training etc.)
- guarantees or insurance schemes.

Budget subsidies

During recent years, the share of *direct* State subsidies for environmental investments amounted to 1-1.3 per cent of GDP. The MEW foresees that it will increase to 3 per cent of GDP over the next 10 years. It was intended for programmes closing uranium and ore mining, and for investment support to municipal environmental protection facilities, mainly waste-water treatment plants and solid waste disposal sites.

In addition to the direct subsidies, the State budget offers the following *indirect* subsidies:

- exemption of taxes on grants for environmental projects (only when the MoE is the receiver or for PHARE projects
- credits/loans without or at low interest (e.g. to the company NEFTOCHIM).

The National Environmental Protection Fund (NEPF)

The Fund was established in 1992. Its management, operations, sources of revenue, areas and types of spending, etc. are contained in the *Regulation for collection, spending and control of the funds under the Environment Protection Funds,* adopted by the Council of Ministers by decree 278/92 and, later, revised decree 168/95.

Until the end of 1997, when it was cancelled, the tax on imported used cars was the Fund's main source of income. In 2000, a new product tax was introduced on all kinds of (inflatable) tyres, except for aeroplanes. Revenues from privatization were received until the end of 1998. Since 1999, such revenue has accrued directly to the State budget. Since 1996, taxes on imported fuel have progressively become the Fund's main source of income (see Table 3.1 below). Enterprises are fined when they discharge pollution above allowed maximum limits. If the enterprise is committed to reaching the standards in a defined period, it is temporarily authorized to discharge pollution above the maximum permitted but has to pay for it, according to a compliance programme approved by the Ministry of Environment and Waters or the Regional Inspectorate. They can apply to have the fines reduced (5-fold) during a defined period.. Finally, administrative fees or fines in connection with MEW or REI services also go to the Fund.

Pollution charges are collected nationwide into non-budgetary accounts with the Ministry of Finance. Of the total, 60 per cent (from payment for permitted emissions) and 70 per cent (from fines for excess emissions) are transferred to the NEPF, and the remaining 40 per cent and 30 per cent to the municipalities (Municipal Environmental Protection Fund). It is not clear how the money is shared out among the individual municipalities, but apparently it is not proportional to the amounts paid up by their own residents.

Table 3.1: Income and expenditures of the National Environmental Protection Fund, 1996-1998

	1996 Million leva	%	1997 Million leva	%	1998 Million leva	%
Income	**1,187**	**100**	**15,703**	**100**	**53,521**	**100**
Tax on imported fuel	298	25	12,305	79	41,466	78
Tax on imported used cars	371	31	-	-	-	-
Funds from privatization	229	19	2,171	14	9,514	18
Pollution charges	76	7	398	2	1,359	2
Administrative taxes/fines/fees	15	1	584	4	554	1
Repayment of previous loans	198	17	245	1	628	1
Projects funded	**1,640**	**100**	**7,262**	**100**	**44,498**	**100**
Grants	872	53	6,706	92	29,755	67
Loans (0 interest)	768	47	556	8	14,743	33

Source: National Environmental Protection Fund.

The NEPF supports the following priority actions:

- establishing and maintaining a national system to monitor and control the environment and emergencies
- purchase of capital and non-material assets for environmental protection (primarily for use by the central laboratory and the Regional Environmental Inspectorates)
- reclamation of flora, recultivation, chemical melioration, biological and integrated plant protection, drainage, landscape protection including protected sites and objects, biodiversity conservation, other pollution prevention and environmental rehabilitation measures
- scientific studies of both a fundamental and an applied character
- scientific or technical services, services for environmental assessment or audits required by MEW
- participation in environment conferences, symposia, seminars, presentations, competitions and other events, education and public awareness raising
- maintenance of the NEPF operations and remuneration of the members of the Board
- NEPF is the basic co-financing institution for environmental investment projects (projects from municipal and private companies).

In supporting these actions, the NEPF may give grants or loans. The income and expenditure structure of the Fund during the past three years, for which figures (rounded) were available, is shown in Table 3.1.

The Municipal Environmental Protection Funds (MEPF)

Parallel to the national fund (the NEPF), funds have been established at the municipal level (MEPF). The two types of fund are governed by the same Regulation (see NEPF above). The funds available to the MEPFs are used to finance basically the priority areas listed above for the NEPF, but on the territory of the respective municipalities. The actual assistance is normally given in the form of smaller grants. However, the regulation does not exclude loans. However, the individual MEPFs are small (e.g. the Sofia MEPF budget for 1999 amounted to DM 100,000) and are thus insignificant as a source for investments. External funds for municipal investments are managed directly by the municipal councils, not by the MEPFs.

The principal sources of income of municipal funds foreseen in the Regulation are:

- a percentage of the municipal taxes for the use of natural resources
- a percentage of the pollution fines collected
- a percentage of the taxes on (permitted) pollution up to the maximum permissible level
- fines imposed for breaking regulations (i.e. municipal regulations listed in the Law of local self-government and administration)
- donations from local or foreign sources.

A waste charge is due for the collection, transport and treatment of waste as well as for the cleaning of public areas in towns. The Municipal Councils set level of the charge annually based on an approved plan. This calculation includes the cost of providing waste containers; collecting and transporting waste to landfills or to other installations for treatment; constructing, maintaining, operating and closing down landfills and other installations for waste treatment; cleaning streets, squares, alleys, parks and other public areas. The charge goes to the municipal budgets.

A water use charge is paid to the water companies. These companies conclude contracts with their customers, in which the conditions for paying the charge are specified. The base for price calculation is the total production cost and treatment of water. It includes the equipment costs, the cost of the water itself; the cost of operating water-supply systems, the extraction, transport, treatment and distribution of water; spare parts; electricity and fuel costs; external services (production activities and services provided by external companies); depreciation; social insurance; and other costs.

The National Trust Ecofund (NTEF)

At the end of 1995, Bulgaria and Switzerland signed a Nature Debt Swap Agreement. The funds were devoted to the implementation of the Bulgarian Biodiversity Conservation Programme, the second phase of which began in 1998 and will continue until 2001. The management of these funds was entrusted to the National Trust Ecofund, which was created in 1996 as an independent institution for this purpose. The wider objective of the Ecofund is to manage funds under debt-for-nature and debt-for-environment swaps, as well as funds provided under other types of agreements with international or national sources, aimed at environmental protection in Bulgaria. To date, no other swap-agreements have been made.

The 1995 swap deal between Bulgaria and Switzerland totalled CHF 22 million, to be committed before the end of 1999. By the end of 1997, commitments of a total of 9.1 billion leva had been made (i.e. approximately CHF 8 million). The fund is trying to attract funds from other foreign donors and to become a managing agency for international financing institutions, but so far without success. NTEF is being considered for managing a World Bank loan to Bulgaria.

Priority areas for support by the NTEF are:

- environmental investment projects of domestic or international priority within Bulgaria
- clean up of pollution and damage

- reduction of air pollution
- protection of biodiversity and protected areas
- purchase and commissioning of ecological equipment
- other activities consistent with the NTEF objectives and financing criteria, e.g. environment-related transfer of technology and know-how, assistance to compliance with international environmental obligations
- other areas as defined/prioritized by the donor/source of revenue.

Within the present Swiss agreement, the support is primarily offered as grants and only exceptionally as soft loans. Future donors/sources via NTEF may offer different types. The NTEF would prefer co-financing schemes with commercial banks, other funds, etc.

Commercial banks

Options for banks to finance environmental investments were effectively closed as a consequence of the serious bank crisis in 1994 to 1996 and the very restrictive regulations subsequently set by the Government. The surviving banks gradually started to recover and to adapt to the new conditions. Further, several commercial banks entered into partnership with foreign banks and started to appoint foreign-trained managers, adapting their operating structures and procedures to meet the new 'banking culture'.

Many of the commercial banks are now ready to offer loans to enterprises. The main features and issues today are:

- The banks appear to have sufficient funds, however, all come from short-term deposits, which cannot be used for long-term loans.
- The banks are not allowed to grant mortgages, enabling long-term, lower-interest loans.
- The banks cannot issue bonds as a basis for capital lending.
- The securities/collateral does not seem to be a major problem, as they are normally offered and taken only in land and buildings, generally evaluated at 125 per cent as required by the current regulation.
- A major obstacle is still the lack of a 'partner culture' between enterprises and the banking sector. The enterprises tend to consider banks as 'deposit institutions' only. The banks' attitude, even when offering a loan, do not appear to provide a 'service', but focus on

'penalties and punishment' if the client defaults.

- The banks (may) find it more attractive to place their excess capital abroad, rather than use it for more risky lending to national companies.
- Given past problems, foreign donors still have only limited trust in local banks. Foreign investors usually insist on an evaluation/confirmation by a foreign bank before accepting a guarantee by a local bank.

International funding

Since 1990, significant projects have been carried out under the Framework Agreement with the European Union, and the PHARE programme, and are coming to an end.   With GEF assistance a number of investment projects were undertaken on the phasing-out of ozone-depleting substances, biodiversity conservation, Danube river protection, Black Sea protection, etc. In 1998, two projects were launched with the World Bank. One concerns the technological conversion of seven enterprises producing refrigerants, including training for technicians handling refrigerants and CFCs. The other is a pilot project for the environmental upgrading of a copper smelter and a privatized refinery (the cost for refinery upgrading is US\$ 25 million).

- The overall EU assistance (in the framework of PHARE) provides support to the transition to a market economy and to meeting the obligations from future EU membership. The environment

Table 3.2: Summary and overview of international assistance to Bulgaria in all sectors including environment, 1995-1998

1 000 US\$

	1995	1996	1997	1998
Grand total	279.86	471.77	1,038.69	1,504.10
Multinational UN system:	*39.92*	*180.49*	*651.38*	*655.80*
GEF		0.21	1.07	1.26
IBRD	38.10	51.80	99.33	195.88
IFC	-	4.91	10.80	108.64
IMF	-	121.44	538.48	347.62
UNDP	0.56	0.43	0.95	2.04
Other UN	1.26	1.70	0.75	0.36
Non-UN:	*125.59*	*210.92*	*261.15*	*699.16*
EU	82.82	137.22	86.86	392.88
EBRD	33.97	46.18	112.99	119.20
EIB	8.80	27.32	60.20	185.07
Other non-UN				2.00
Bilateral	*114.35*	*80.37*	*107.84*	*147.53*
Austria	0.34	0.70	1.74	1.36
Belgium	0.88	0.76	1.10	1.26
Denmark	0.33	0.79	2.78	2.32
France	0.97	2.19	1.97	2.57
Germany	10.36	12.12	11.98	13.40
Greece			4.07	
Japan	57.43	13.39	11.15	64.43
Netherlands	10.09	1.63	3.12	6.12
Spain			100.00	1.06
Switzerland	5.59	14.02	9.67	6.94
UK	3.20	3.78	4.03	5.74
USA	25.00	30.49	55.79	41.29
Other bilateral	0.17	0.51	0.35	1.04
Foreign Red Cross organisations			*18.322*	*0.33*

Source: UNDP Report 1998.

sector is one of several receiving PHARE support. The overall PHARE programme has, therefore, a large number of budget lines, by sector or type of project. Three budget lines are the main sources of funding for environmental projects.

- The yearly allocation from the *PHARE National Programme* to the environmental sector (the environment sector allocation) is agreed via yearly memoranda between the EU and the Government of Bulgaria. The size of the yearly allocation depends on the current priorities of the EU Commission and the Bulgarian Government. The Strategy Department in the MEW is the managing and implementing agency.

The terms and profile of planned spending is, in principle, agreed year by year, in the form of the intended share for grants or loans, and through the planned division for capital investment/technical assistance/other types of financing, depending on the national programme for the year. In the 1990-1995 period, the support was primarily for technical assistance to technical project studies, feasibility studies, monitoring and data collection/field equipment, information systems and IT equipment, programme management, training, public awareness raising, etc. All activities were prerequisites for identifying and preparing subsequent investment projects. It is foreseen that the focus will shift to areas critical for implementing the EU environmental *acquis* in the coming years.

In principle, the PHARE National Programme may offer all types of financial assistance: grants, soft and other loans, guarantees, interest subsidies, equity, etc. However, in practice only grants and loans have so far been given. Grants can only be given to State institutions and non-profit NGOs, but not to private companies, in order not to distort the market mechanisms. PHARE support will increasingly become conditional on co-financing from other sources (e.g. commercial banks, self-financing by the applicant). Accordingly, PHARE support cannot go beyond a ceiling percentage of total project cost.

- The *Cross Border Cooperation Programme (CBCP)* is the second budget line of PHARE with an environmental sector allocation. This programme is specifically intended to support projects having a transboundary environmental effect between EU-member countries on the one hand and non-EU member countries on the other. In the case of Bulgaria, the programme may therefore be available for projects in the Bulgarian/Greek border regions. The size of the 'environment' budget allocation from this programme is also decided on a yearly basis, depending on agreement between the countries involved and the EC. The implementing authority in Bulgaria is the Ministry of Regional Development and Public Works (MRDPW).

The CBCP priorities for border regions are:

- Transport infrastructure improvements
- Water supply, telecommunications, gas and electricity transmission networks and other utilities
- Economic development, especially support to small and medium-sized enterprises (SMEs), business info centres, etc.
- New agricultural processes, sanitary and veterinary control
- Social and health services, vocational training.

The programme is thus available to help fund waste-water treatment systems, monitoring of river water, nuclear safety, waste treatment, and erosion protection. The CBCP is exclusively oriented towards investment projects, undertaken by border municipalities and/or State institutions. Private companies cannot apply. Assistance takes the form of grants exempt of duties and taxes, preferably co-financed from other sources.

- The third budget line available in PHARE with an environment sector allocation is the *Instrument for Structural Policies for pre-Accession (ISPA)*. For several reasons - one being a wish to allow larger projects of greater impact - the EU recently decided to create a special budget line for large-scale projects. The initial activities - now in progress in Bulgaria - comprise identification of large-scale projects, setting up the implementation structures and resources and complete the formalities for signing the financial memorandum for the first year's allocation (2000). Currently, the Bulgarian ISPA programme comprises the two sectors transport and environment. The national coordination vis-à-vis the EC is the responsibility of MRDPW, with MEW and

Box 3.1: The environmental priorities of ISPA

The financial instrument for infrastructure in the environment sector will begin functioning in 2000. The environmental priorities of ISPA focus on three sectors: waste management, air quality and water quality, aiming to bring these sectors into compliance with EU requirements. An estimate of the total investment expenditures necessary for the 2000-2006 period largely surpasses the budget for the three sectors envisaged under the National Development Plan. ISPA funds will make up the difference.

The priority projects selected for ISPA financing are:

- *Ambient air quality:* Setting-up of a desulphurization installation at "Maritsa-East 2" thermal power plant.
- *Water quality:* Thirty-six WWTP priority projects for cities with over 10,000 inhabitants were selected, some of them existing WWTPs that will undergo reconstruction (in Sofia, Plovdiv, Varna, Veliko Turnovo, Razgrad, Sliven and Primorsko). Others are new urban WWTPs – already under construction or about to begin construction. ISPA funds will be concentrated on those projects which have not yet commenced, while the other projects continue to be financed from public funds (the National budget, NEPF, municipal budgets).
- *Waste management:* The three projects proposed – a national centre for the treatment of hazardous waste, a number of regional municipal waste disposal sites, and an installation for the treatment and safe disposal of waste in Sofia, are priority investment projects in the National Programme for Waste Management.

Table 3.2: Summary and overview of international assistance to Bulgaria in all sectors
including environment, 1995-1998

1 000 US$

	1995	1996	1997	1998
Grand total	279.86	471.77	1,038.69	1,504.10
Multinational UN system:	*39.92*	*180.49*	*651.38*	*655.80*
GEF		0.21	1.07	1.26
IBRD	38.10	51.80	99.33	195.88
IFC	-	4.91	10.80	108.64
IMF	-	121.44	538.48	347.62
UNDP	0.56	0.43	0.95	2.04
Other UN	1.26	1.70	0.75	0.36
Non-UN:	*125.59*	*210.92*	*261.15*	*699.16*
EU	82.82	137.22	86.86	392.88
EBRD	33.97	46.18	112.99	119.20
EIB	8.80	27.32	60.20	185.07
Other non-UN				2.00
Bilateral	*114.35*	*80.37*	*107.84*	*147.53*
Austria	0.34	0.70	1.74	1.36
Belgium	0.88	0.76	1.10	1.26
Denmark	0.33	0.79	2.78	2.32
France	0.97	2.19	1.97	2.57
Germany	10.36	12.12	11.98	13.40
Greece			4.07	
Japan	57.43	13.39	11.15	64.43
Netherlands	10.09	1.63	3.12	6.12
Spain			100.00	1.06
Switzerland	5.59	14.02	9.67	6.94
UK	3.20	3.78	4.03	5.74
USA	25.00	30.49	55.79	41.29
Other bilateral	0.17	0.51	0.35	1.04
Foreign Red Cross organisations			*18.322*	*0.33*

Source: UNDP Report 1998.

Ministry of Transport as the implementing authorities for the environment and transport sector projects, respectively.

The Bulgarian Government and the EU have identified a series of large-scale priority projects. These projects will be gradually implemented over a 5-year period, thus averaging 7 per year, and absorb all the ISPA funding available within the period. Each project - or group of projects being implemented as 'one ISPA project' - shall have a total project cost of not less than 5 million euro. ISPA funds a maximum of 75 per cent of the total cost, exceptionally 85 per cent. The type of support depends on the overall financing possibilities and options in each case (especially co-financing and recipient financing) and can take the form of a grant, loan, etc.

- The United Nations Development Programme (UNDP) provides a central coordination mechanism for the planning, organization and provision of technical assistance by the entire United Nations system. UNDP is thus a focal point between the Government of Bulgaria and the ultimate provider of the actual project funding from all United Nations sources. UNDP itself provides only grants for technical assistance and capacity building in connection with development/implementation of programmes coordinated by it. At present these include:

  - Climate and energy efficiency measures from the Global Environment Facility (GEF)
  - Ecological monitoring and pollution control of the Maritsa River basin (project completed)
  - Ecological monitoring of the Black Sea (maritime oil pollution in the Varna region/ project completed)
  - Environmental management of the Black Sea (regional project)
  - Environmental management of the Danube River basin (regional project)

Only national administrations (governments/ministries/State institutions) and NGOs are eligible. The assistance for the completed projects totalled some 250,000 to 300,000 US dollars, and the implementing agency was the MEW.

Two GEF projects are being implemented through UNDP. The development of an energy-efficiency strategy to limit greenhouse-gas (GHG) emissions (see list above) is a fully-fledged GEF project valued at 2.5 million US dollars. It targets municipalities, which are seen as the critical level of administration in this problem area. The project includes the establishment of a municipal energy-efficiency network and three demonstration schemes. At present, 31 municipalities participate in the project compared with 26 municipalities at the outset. A second GEF project establishes a funding opportunity for meeting Bulgarian obligations with regard to biodiversity conservation. Although US$ 154,000 was spent on preparing the biodiversity action plan, continuation of the project is dependent on the determination of national priorities.

The regional cooperation projects on Danube and Black Sea protection receive funds from the EU Phare programme and GEF. In addition, UNDP also financed a 'Capacity 21' project, with the creation, after the Rio Summit, of a 'Capacity 21 Task Force' in the Ministry for Regional Development and Public Works, and local agendas 21 in two municipalities. In the initial phase, around US$ 700,000 were spent on these initiatives.

- The World Bank pursues the overall objectives of advancing economic growth and reducing poverty. The Bank is raising and channelling international loans. Its environmental activities can be divided into (a) providing general technical assistance to national governments and institutions to prepare, update and implement national environment strategies and actions plans, and (b) to undertake 'banking activities', i.e. processing loan applications, identifying/raising/compiling funds, formalizing international agreements, servicing loan agreements etc.

The spectrum of World Bank support is very wide. In principle it relates to all social and environmental dimensions of development, and their relationship to economic and technical factors. Normally the loan activities will have a direct link to the priorities identified and agreed in the country's environmental strategies and action plans for sustainable development, elaborated with assistance from the World Bank. When a World Bank loan package eventually has been agreed upon, the individual projects to be financed under the loan must undergo a rigorous application and acceptance procedure before the project is approved and funds can be released.

Technical assistance is financed directly via the overall World Bank budget, in turn covered by contributions from member countries. The actual World Bank loans come from funds issued in world financial markets or from World Bank member countries. The World Bank lends to governments or private entities, to the latter only against government guarantees. In some cases (and provided that good and transparent management can be assured), the World Bank may allow the loan to be transferred to a government-controlled fund, for issuing grants or loans according to the regulations of the fund (see Chapter 1, the section on the privatization process).

In 1995 a special *Water Loan Project* agreement was concluded between Bulgaria and the World Bank, specifically designed to assist the restructuring and modernization of water companies or utilities. The loan amounted to US$ 98 million. The specific environmental aim was to improve the health and environmental conditions in urban areas and to conserve water resources. The loan is managed by a special 'Water Project Management Unit' in the MRDPW. All projects concerning water pollution prevention or waste-water treatment are eligible. The secondary priorities are:

- rehabilitation or upgrading of water and sewage facilities
- water efficiency and reduction of water losses
- procurement of related goods, equipment and materials
- civil works, installation and turnkey contracts.

Only registered water and sewage companies can apply for loans and they should be at least 49 per cent owned by municipalities. State-owned companies are not eligible as applicants. The World Bank loan can in principle only be re-issued in the form of loans, based on an adjusted central bank rediscounting rate, generally over a 13-year period. Grants may be allowed, but only for the preparation of tender documents for the specific project being proposed or applied for.

- The European Bank for Reconstruction and Development (EBRD) is a multinational institution (not equal to a commercial bank), with the purpose of assisting the countries of central and eastern Europe in their transition to a market economy. Its shareholders are countries (national banks), the EU and the European Investment Bank (EIB). Considering its high-rated group of shareholders, the EBRD is able to raise funds at very favourable terms on the international capital market.

  EBRD gives high priority to projects with a 'multiplier effect', i.e. demonstration projects with benefits to the local economy, mobilizing co-financing, facilitating technology transfer and management skills, encouraging joint ventures for foreign investors, etc. EBRD operates in both the public and private sectors.

  In principle, EBRD offers a wide range of financial instruments, from normal lending, syndicated loans, guarantees, to equity investment and advisory/consultancy services. Grants may be provided for technical assistance or project preparation from its Technical Cooperation Fund Programme. Loans should normally be at least ECU 5 million. They are given at market interest rates, but do not require State or foreign guarantees. Co-financing is normally required.

- The European Investment Bank (EIB) is generally interested in financing projects in the Bulgarian energy sector. Currently, EIB is financing projects for the Bulgarian National Electric Company. EIB requires State or private guarantees, the latter to be provided by an international A-1 bank, with representation in Bulgaria. EIB provides up to 50 per cent of the project investment, in the form of loans of 10-15 million euro. Generally the terms are:

  - 20 to 25-year maturity for a State-guaranteed loan
  - 10 to 15-year maturity for loans against private guarantee
  - grace periods are normally 25 per cent of the maturity period
  - the interest will be close to the market rate

- if co-financed by the State, the conditions will be more favourable
- small projects may be financed via a 'global loan line', operated by HYPO Bank, Munich

- A large number of countries are offering bilateral assistance to Bulgaria, both to State institutions or municipalities and to private enterprises. For example, a number of environmentally relevant projects are being coordinated by sectoral institutions and funded by international partners. The Economy Ministry, for example, manages a pollution control project in Bulgarian tanneries, and coordinates the introduction of cleaner production in a non-ferrous metal plant in Elisejna. The Energy and Energy Efficiency Agency is heading a project for the abatement of sulphur at the country's largest coal-fired power plant (Maritza-Iztok 2). Table 3.2 includes the major bilateral donors during 1995-1998, all of which remain open for support applications.

Contrary to the general principle for EU support, which normally proceeds from a mutually agreed maximum budget to allocations to projects meeting certain criteria, the bilateral donors generally start by inviting project applications, which they may then finance. The priorities funded vary widely from donor to donor between environmental sectors, area of the country, and type of beneficiary. The support may be either direct in the form of grants, loans or co-financing, but is most often - especially from the smaller donors – in the form of indirect financing by providing technical assistance, equipment, etc.

Some donors may have a preference for certain types of supplies (e.g. technical assistance in certain areas like institutional development, project preparation, etc.), or for equipment (specific air cleaning equipment, equipment for monitoring and/or analysis, etc.). A concern of most donors is being able to identify their own individual support and being able to confirm its successful completion. Therefore, many donors prefer to fully support a project of limited size, rather than to participate with other donors in a larger project. However, as smaller projects do not have the same impact, there is a clear trend towards co-financing with other donors. In this case, participation by the EU is often preferred, as it may add to project quality and transparency. A complete and qualified project proposal in accordance with the donor's

requirements is a must for all donors. This includes full and qualified justification of environmental, technical and economic benefits.

Most donors require - as part of the project proposal - convincing documentation of the readiness of the project to start and/or to be implemented, depending on the nature of the project. Additionally, it must be documented that the authority responsible for the implementation (the counterpart) has sufficient resources, in terms of capacity and quality.

Most donors require also active and qualified participation by the beneficiary in the process, at the beneficiary's own expense. Also, the beneficiary may be required to provide other input (possibly in kind) to ensure successful implementation, for example paying for external technical expertise for analysis (e.g. when EIA is required). Finally, all donors require confirmation that the proposed project is in line with (or does not conflict with) national, regional or local policies or plans. This requirement suggests that all Bulgarian applications ought to pass through the MEW.

3.2 Possible developments of financing instruments

Broad characteristics of current instruments

The possible sources of funds and financing mechanisms are well identified and well known to the MEW, and most of them are used (see section 3.1 above). Many of the existing possibilities, not least the bilateral cooperation, are far from exhausted. The question is, therefore, not so much to find new sources of funding, but rather to develop, combine and refine the sources or mechanisms already known, by creating the conditions for extending their use. This section deals with increasing the finance base, whereas section 3.3 is devoted to the problems of 'institutional limitations' and 'improved bankability of project applications'.

The financing instruments currently in use have been designed more as taxes and sanctions to raise revenue, than to encourage a change in environmental behaviour. This is especially true as regards consumer fees, which are regularly fixed per household, or calculated per square metre of floor space, etc., and so not affected by the quantity or volume of use of the service. Furthermore, as consumer fees are paid into State accounts (even though a percentage of the collected total is later returned to the municipalities), the consumers do not always recognize the link between the fees they pay and the environmental situation in their municipality. However, water meters are now gradually being installed, especially in connection with the privatization of the water utilities. No doubt this will reduce the volumes of both water use and sewage water.

In some interviews during the EPR review mission it was pointed out that the present formula used to redistribute part of the collected fees to municipalities was felt to be unfair and counterproductive by those municipalities that made special efforts to reduce the water use, sewage and waste. The bigger the reduction they achieved, the smaller the amount of money returned from the central government. The present system is claimed to favour the municipalities that do little or nothing, instead of favouring those that make improvements through their own efforts and investments.

The company NEFTOCHIM is responsible for the collection of all fuel taxes and payments into the State accounts. The company is now privatized. The close connection between NEFTOCHIM and the Government may jeopardize the actual and timely flow of the fuel revenues to NEPF. Previously, the NEPF experienced large delays in receiving the related revenues, and had to work on what is called a 'physically received only basis'. Further, the major part of the expected revenue in 1999 was recently converted to a loan from NEPF for a future investment project in NEFTOCHIM, on very favourable terms.

Options for the development of individual instruments

Consumer fees for use of natural resources. The levels of fees are set in national laws and municipal decisions. However, it is also important to analyse to which extent the fees are actually used for environmental investments, or for the general needs of the State budget. The acceptance by the public of a possible rise in the fees is probably directly linked to the transparency of the payments and their subsequent use. Higher fees must be justified by visible improvements, preferably within the local community.

The present tariff systems do not necessarily ensure that the fee reflects the cost of the service. These services need to be fully costed, including all maintenance, amortization and interest costs for loans and reinvestments. This problem is probably shrinking as more utilities are privatized. The calculations also have to be transparent, as, in the past, fees may have included general mark-ups for overall revenue purposes. Such transparency may make fee levels more readily acceptable by the public.

Correct determination of fee payments. Enforcement of fee payment is not only a technical issue, it also requires sufficient and appropriate information systems and other controlling instruments. Such instruments are needed to avoid for instance a reduction in total fees by manipulating the figures on which the fees are based (e.g. for enterprises the amount of solid waste produced, water intake, volume of sewage water, etc.).

Collection system for fines and fees. While the number of fines may have increased, the system for collecting the fines due still needs to ensure timely and full payment. One improvement may be to create additional and heavy fines, if the original payments are not effected in due time. The same problem of full and timely payments may also apply to the general collection of consumer fees.

Privatization of utility services. The privatization agreement should oblige the future private operator, whether national or foreign, to finance the required investments for rehabilitation or new construction. In exchange, the future contractor should receive a long-term contract and should be given the possibility of charging realistic fees.

Privatization and/or sale of municipal non-utility assets. In several interviews during the EPR review mission, it was stated that many municipalities (including Sofia) own enterprises, hotels/restaurants, buildings not used for municipal administration, licences, etc., which, if realized at market values, represent substantial capital funds. These could be used for municipal, including environmental, investments. It was also noted that, where assets had been disposed of, the sales price had often appeared unrealistically low and non-transparent, even though the law required independent valuation. The existing laws allow municipalities to privatize and sell their assets, but they are not required to do so - for instance, to self-finance their environmental investments.

Use of municipal non-utility assets as loan security. If municipalities do not wish to privatize or otherwise dispose of assets that are not a direct part of the municipal administration, these assets may be used as a guarantee for loans in commercial banks. Interviews held during the EPR review mission clearly indicated that the municipalities would have few problems in raising loans for their investments in this way.

Municipal bonds. According to a new law, municipalities may now issue bonds for sale on the capital market. The prospective buyers seem to be the new pension funds, insurance companies, etc. Further analysis of the possibilities opened by this new provision is required.

Mandatory co-financing by beneficiaries. Until now, it has not been mandatory for the beneficiaries of investment grants and/or loans to participate in funding through co-financing arrangements. To a small extent this has nevertheless occurred, with the required co-financing often provided by third-party funds and sources and not by the beneficiary. With a view to gradually building investment mechanisms based on market conditions, it is necessary to start obliging the beneficiaries to participate, either with own means or via commercial banks. Recently, municipalities have started to receive such support and are learning how to administrate such projects.

Commercial banking. During the past decade, most (if not all) environmental investments have naturally been in the public sector, i.e. by ministries, State institutions and municipalities. This has had the following serious consequences:

- 'Environmental investments' have very much been limited to, and mainly perceived as, technical and institutional improvements in the public sector only. A clear conclusion from many interviews conducted during the EPR review mission was that 'environmental improvements and investments' are still primarily seen as a Ministry or State problem. The fact that commercial sector investments into environmental improvements are equally critical, if the industry is to survive under international market conditions, has not yet dawned on the enterprises and the general public.

- The above perception - combined with the virtual non-existence of commercial banks under the previous regime - has seriously delayed the emergence of 'partnership' relations between industry and banks. The industries felt that the banks were not interested in cooperating, and the banks, on their side, only saw risks in cooperating with industry. The recent bank crisis has further delayed the development of such a new partnership culture.

- The combined effect of the above has been that the Bulgarian banking sector is not yet recognized as an important funding source, and the efforts to start practical pilot cooperation from the side of the public authorities appear limited. As long as public institutions maintain a negative opinion of the banks, private industry will probably hesitate to make serious efforts on its own to cooperate with the banks, and will tend to rely first (if not only) on foreign assistance.

The commercial banking sector appears to be opening up. Even if the banking regulations may be further improved, regulatory obstacles to increased cooperation do not appear to exist in the short term. A very first step towards a full incorporation of commercial banks into environmental funding mechanisms might be for the National Environmental Protection Fund to insist on co-financing by local banks.

Creation of a national loan-guarantee scheme. Private enterprises, when negotiating guarantees, securities or collateral with commercial banks, may be faced with discouraging bank requirements. These tend to be demanding, as the banks not only need to consider their risks, but are also more interested in production-oriented than environmental investments. Their focus on risks also limits the banks' involvement as a financial development partner for the enterprise.

The establishment of a loan-guarantee bank or institution, which could provide guarantees for qualified projects to the commercial bank giving the loan could help to alleviate bank risks. By operating a formal scheme - managing multiple guarantees - the risk for the individual loan will be spread and more easily absorbed. Priorities should of course be given to good projects, but which have difficulties in raising alternative guarantees. Such a scheme would normally be operated by a bank with State participation. If so, it is likely that international financial assistance could be obtained to form the capital base for the guarantee institution.

Further development of the NEPF. According to its statutes, the NEPF has the possibility of developing alternative sources of finance for raising and generating income or capital: changing grants to revolving loans, and demanding interest on loans, possibly softened. These possibilities have not been pursued until now. One of the main functions of the NEPF in the short term should, however, be to develop its existing 'cash' sources.

The NEPF could also be very valuable as a focal mechanism between international (bilateral) donors and enterprises pursuing environmental projects. Furthermore, the NEPF could play an important role in involving the commercial banks in co-financing arrangements.

International sources. The United Nations and IFI sources are fully known and used by the Government, when necessary. Possible problems may be related to general economic development in Bulgaria, national priority issues, political issues, guarantees, and the availability of professional resources to deal with the international institutions, including in the preparation of qualified projects.

Likewise, European Union programmes and applicable budget lines are known and used as applicable. The existence of a Delegation of the European Commission in Bulgaria ensures a two-way flow of information. The possible problems relate first and foremost to the 'institutional capacity' of MEW to prepare projects, manage the implementation in strict accordance with the EC rules, and ensure sufficient and qualified absorbing capacity of the final beneficiary. See also below.

Bilateral sources of environmental funding are far from exhausted. As noted above, all bilateral donors have their own set of priorities and conditions. However, the major problem is claimed to be the lack of properly prepared and well presented project proposals. The problem has three sides:

- The donor's side: Basically all donors have their own individual application forms, standards for presenting details and required supporting documentation, etc. Furthermore, donors do not always disclose sufficient practical details on their priorities, formats and other conditions, making it difficult for applicants to prepare their applications accordingly.

- The applicant's side: The main problems are (a) an insufficient or incorrect application format or procedure required by donors, (b) a too limited project vision, not normally

including a strategic and development purpose, but simply that of an ordinary 'activity financing', and (c) communication barriers in terms of both language and business or management culture. For example, applicants often focus on technical issues and tend to ignore financial and economic issues, including sustainability, as relevant for a project to be accepted.

- The approving government's side: The overriding problem at the time of the EPR review mission seemed to be that the applicant rarely knew from which source he might eventually receive support, e.g. an EC programme, the NEPF, other State sources or a foreign bilateral donor. As each source has its own requirements for applications, the applicant is frequently unable to present and tailor an application to the requirements of the ultimate source.

All involved authorities must have sufficient capacity and qualifications to handle, process and decide on applications. If a bilateral donor is identified as a potential financing source, the authorities may need to undertake a certain amount of processing of the application. In addition, they must have a clear-cut, well defined and published procedure for receiving applications and providing feedback on them to the applicants. The overall procedure requires 'process orientation', structures, and qualifications within the involved institutions, permitting delegation of sufficient authority to the operational managers.

Debt-for-environment swaps. Such arrangements between the Bulgarian Government and a bilateral debtor mean that Bulgaria's debts are converted - in full or in part – into an obligation on the Bulgarian Government to spend the corresponding amount on national environmental investments, normally through a fund. The only existing swap arrangement was made with Switzerland. It is managed by the National Trust Ecofund. Assuming that Bulgaria is in fact paying off or making budget reserves to service the debts, a swap arrangement is extremely favourable to the country. If more swaps are agreed in the future, it may be an advantage to entrust their management to one institution. This would generally allow for more professional management, transparency and cumulative impact.

Attracting foreign private investors. This option is, of course, well known. However, indications are that the general lack of communication between the authorities and donors is also a limiting factor in matching Bulgarian enterprises with potential foreign investors. Even if a connection is made, the lack of official interest and the bureaucracy appear to be discouraging. If there were a dynamic coordinating assisting body, significant progress could be made. Furthermore, the Internet may also help enterprises establishing contact with donors and potential sources of finance.

3.3   Institutional and 'bankability' issues

Institutional practices

Creating a positive climate for environmental investments is a complex development and not only a matter of raising cash. Many factors need to contribute, with positive input in the same direction. The most fundamental requirement is that the institutions, the industries and the general public should broadly agree about what environmental investments are needed, what their relation is to the social and economic difficulties of the country, and what the priorities are.

Meeting the EU directives and requirements for membership is the national objective most often cited. A more complete system of social objectives will undoubtedly emerge. It may be important to prepare this complete system by starting to raise the visibility of the results that were obtained from past and ongoing environment investments. For the time being, it is still considered the State's problem to improve the environment and make the required investments. Both enterprises and the general public need to develop an understanding of their own role in this regard.

The active participation of entrepreneurs is essential to the renewal process. Two major variables influence this participation, institutional procedures in relation to entrepreneurial activity, and the general status of entrepreneurial activities. Institutional bureaucracy and institutional conservatism do not change fast. Most institutional structures are still overwhelmingly political and not yet fully geared to the concept of institutional service. The status of entrepreneurial activities is widely assessed as being very low. It seems that many qualified Bulgarian entrepreneurs are leaving the country because their businesses face limitations and obstacles.

Over the past decade, many old industries have disappeared – a process that has probably not yet come to an end. In parallel, however, positive challenges develop for new industries. This is the case not only in information technology, but also in environmental protection. Industry still needs to take up this challenge at full scale.

Incentives for investments are, of course, very much linked to the economic situation, the expectations of improvements, financial/regulatory restraints on the economy etc. The situation in the recent past has not been favourable to investments, not least as a result of the bank crisis of 1996 and 1997. It seems that the successful application of a currency board system has started to bring confidence back. The careful monitoring of the situation should make initiatives for private environmental protection investments possible at the earliest possible date.

Bankability

In this chapter, the term is used to cover all activities - from initial application until successful physical completion of the project. The reason for this extended definition is that, today, Bulgaria is experiencing a number of significant practical problems, besides the quality of the application dossier, which prevent, limit or delay projects, especially when aiming at bilateral donors.

The easiest presentation of the problems is in terms of the structure of a normal project cycle. It includes the following phases:

- *Project identification.* The project idea or vision or purpose normally appears either at the applicant's own initiative, or as a result of a call for applications by a donor.

- *Application/project preparation.* This covers the description of the project in the required detail and with all supporting analysis and documentation. Ideally an application would have two steps:

Step 1 leads to the initial overall description - usually called 'project fiche' - as a basis for a first screening for eligibility, for formal completeness and/or for initial identification of a potential financing source.

Step 2 produces the full project application dossier, with all details, analysis, assessments, financial projections, supporting documents including permits, etc. NEPF and NETF have formalized - but differing - application forms and guidelines.

- *Application submission, receipt, registration, and acknowledgement of receipt by the relevant authority.* This refers to the precise procedure to be followed by any applicant, including the address to which the application has to be sent, the detailed procedures by the receiving authority including a mandatory acknowledgement of the receipt of the application to the applicant, by whom it is being handled and when a reply can be expected. For environmental projects, this authority will normally be the MEW. Even if the application is for a specific bilateral donor, it (normally) has to pass via MEW for approval and/or endorsement.

- *Application processing.* This covers the precise and well-defined procedure for processing the application after registration. In the first screening, eligibility according to strategies, priorities, formal grounds, competitive ranking, financing source or donor. If the application passes this screening, the processing of the full project dossier can proceed, with evaluation of all details, assessments and analysis of technical, environmental and financial aspects, the implementing time schedule and organization, the completion of the financing package, etc.

- *Final project assessment and decision by donor.* The application data - both for the first and second screening in the preceding phase - are (normally) provided by the applicant or by technical assistance to the applicant. The donor's technical and project managing staff 'process the application'. The recommendations from this phase are presented to the donor's political level for final approval.

- *Implementation activities.* This phase covers all the physical activities following the final approval of the project (tender preparation and tendering process, contracting with the successful contractor, detailed design/development of the project, physical implementation with works, equipment procurements, installation, etc., any supporting activities like training, preparation of instruction manuals, testing, etc., reporting to all parties involved, and financial control, incl. contract management as relevant).

- *Follow-up.* This covers *ex post* evaluations to confirm that objectives were realized, and statement of the good and bad lessons learned.

The principal parties normally involved in the above project cycle are:

- *the applicant,* responsible for preparing the application with all required details and supporting documents.

- *external technical assistants and consultants,* for supporting the applicant and all other parties (including MEW) in preparations and evaluations, EIAs, financial analysis, etc. The technical assistance may be both national and international.

- *the Ministry of Environment and Waters (MEW)* is involved at five levels. The Strategy Department serves as the implementing agency for EU and other international projects, except bilateral projects. It receives and registers all applications and identifies the (possible) financing source. The Technical Department evaluates and confirms technical solutions included in the project. The political level of the Ministry takes decisions on which projects to support. The NEPF Executive Office handles applications redirected by the Strategy Department to NEPF for financing. The NEPF Management Committee approves projects proposed to the NEPF Operating Office.

- *the multinational donors/financiers: World Bank, EBRD, other IFIs, UNDP, etc.* process and approve projects through their own technical assistance units. This process may involve both offices in Bulgaria, as well as other authorities outside Bulgaria.

- *the bilateral donors* process and approve projects through their own technical assistance units. This process may concern both offices in Bulgaria as well as home-country authorities.

- *the Delegation of the European Commission* endorses or approves, after checking, projects (documentation), tenders, contracts, compliance with EC rules and requirements, etc.

The major bankability problems

The above wide definition of 'bankability' makes it possible to highlight a number of problems, which have a negative impact on the financing of environmental investments.

- *Lack of knowledge of available financing possibilities and opportunities.* Even if efforts are being made by the competent ministerial services to inform applicants of funding possibilities, there still seems to be a considerable lack of 'useful' information. In particular, it is noted that most enterprises do not know how to communicate with donors.

- *Lack of knowledge about projects suitable for funding.* In the same way in which the applicants lack information on financing opportunities, donors lack information and feedback on existing projects that might meet their financing criteria. The yearly donor meeting appears insufficient and far too static to produce this information. Furthermore, projects presented there have been subject to a prior selection process, with which the donors are unfamiliar.

- *Lack of uniform application procedures.* The overriding problem in this connection is that all donors have different application forms (if any at all), different guidelines for contents and detailing of applications, for formats and presentation, etc. Furthermore, some donors may request an initial project fiche, to be followed by a full application only if the project fiche is accepted. Others prefer full-scale documentation already at the time of first submission. The result is that, unless the applicant knows the donor (financing source) beforehand, he is in fact unable to prepare a qualified, 'bankable' application. He simply does not know which forms and which rules he should apply for his application. Further, even if the source of potential funding is known, only very general guidelines are available to the applicant, if any at all.

- *Lack of knowledge by applicants about donors' priorities and focus areas.* Some donors are flexible in their choice of projects, as long as these meet their internal priorities and conditions. Also, they may prefer the applications to reflect the substantive merits of the projects rather than be too tailor-made to the conditions. While this is of course very justified, it makes it more difficult for the applicant to fully understand the donor's requirements for documentation.

- *Applicants' limited project preparation skills and resources, leading to deficient project proposals.* Reminiscent of the old regime, some enterprises do not yet consider economic issues as important as technical ones. The notion of strategic visions and business development culture is still limited. In addition, the enterprises have limited staff resources,

language skills, etc. Finally, applicants may also lack knowledge of the rules and procedures for tendering, and other general requirements to be fulfilled in order to ensure transparency.

- *Lack of a clear procedure for the submission of applications, their receipt and registration.* In principle, all applications are to be submitted to the MEW. However, several interviews during the EPR review mission produced the impression that the form and procedures for submission, including the precise addressee within MEW, are unclear to the applicants. Since applicants, as a rule, do not receive any acknowledgement of receipt of their application by the MEW with a reference number, they often feel their applications get lost. A general feeling among applicants is that you have to hand over the application personally to somebody high up in the hierarchy in MEW.

- *Insufficient project handling resources at MEW.* The handling of the increasing number of projects, and the need for interaction with many donors, has put a strain on MEW resources in this area, especially outside the NEPF. The most critical issues are:

  - The majority of staff has, naturally in a technical ministry like MEW, a technical academic background. There is a lack of general management, administration, planning and economic skills at the operational levels. This last issue is especially serious as it limits the ability for financial or economic evaluations.
  - There is a lack of well-defined standard procedures, manuals and guidelines for project preparation, in written form. Most procedures today are person-based and there is thus no 'institutional memory', when staff leaves the MEW. The absence of an efficient computerized project management system, describing all steps in the project cycle, including financial and contract management, makes the lack of written manuals even more serious. Also, it undermines the transparency of operations and decisions.
  - Throughout the project cycle, there is a constant need for decisions of an operational nature. However, due to the above lack of written agreed procedures and the limited delegation of authority from the political levels, most decisions - even simple ones - need to be taken at high

levels, i.e. by the minister or a deputy minister. This influences not only the time used for processing applications, but also limits the feeling of responsibility, public service orientation and involvement at lower levels of the Ministry. It may favour a 'fire-fighting and crisis-oriented' management of projects.

- *Insufficient overall coordination of strategies, priorities and financing sources.* The identification, coordination and planning of the many combinations of projects and financing, within the overall NEAP strategies and according to annual priorities, is an enormous task, which MEW is trying to achieve. However, in the opinion of some of the donors, there should be more transparency and openness in this planning to encourage donors to increase their financing.

3.4   Conclusions and recommendations

The Bulgarian Ministry of Environment and Waters is making admirable and energetic efforts to swiftly improve the conditions for successful environmental management in the country, primarily through forceful transposition of the requirements for EU accession. Much has been achieved, but much also remains to be done. The aim of the present chapter was to look at the mechanisms for financing environmental protection investments, which are badly needed, if the country's environmental conditions are to improve.

The overall conclusion from the EPR project is that two categories of problems exist for the mobilization of funding sources. The first relates to the increase in the number of sources available (including possibilities for their extension with the help of new financing mechanisms) and their more systematic use. The future environmental investments will indeed require an increasing amount of financing, and new sources are clearly important. However, the potentially available new sources – or new financing instruments - are known to the Government and the MEW, and their use is more a political rather than a practical issue. Furthermore, problems of a more general nature also influence the current 'investment climate and possibilities' negatively. The message therefore is that the development of more financing sources in the short and medium term needs to be considered in a broader context, and not only as a purely monetary issue.

The major problems for the short and medium term - likely to grow unless tackled – appear to be located in the second problem area. They can be described as institutional limitations preventing the full and adequate use of existing funds, as well as the submission of qualified projects for funding. It is therefore suggested to concentrate in the very near future on improving existing project handling mechanisms. The most important general deficiencies of the existing system results in the following unfavourable situation:

- The present system of submitting, receiving, processing and managing project proposals - eventually approved projects - is insufficient and creates delays, bottlenecks, a lack of transparency, delays in spending of available funds and in the release of new funds.
- The many institutions involved in the overall process tend to focus only on themselves with little regard for communication, providing and sharing information at the operational levels in Bulgaria, and with foreign donors. The change towards a 'public service culture' needs to be accelerated.
- Project management and implementation require professional skills in general, and in specific project management in particular, notably in the areas of economics, financing, organization, informatics, communication and (especially) English. Such qualifications are needed even in technical ministries.
- The concentration of all decision-making in the involved State institutions at the highest hierarchical levels creates delays and unnecessarily leads to crisis management. It promotes the general perception that applications need personal support at high level to be successful.

By far the biggest problem today is that (apart from NEPF and NETF) there is no standard format for project applications. Further, in many cases, the applicant does not know the potential source of finance for his specific project. Therefore, the applicant is on the one hand unable to prepare an application, meeting (the possible) donor's requirements. On the other hand, the potential donor is unable to process the application (if received by him at all), due to the non-conformance with the donor's requirements. The only way to solve this dual issue is to develop a standard format for the initial stage of a project application, i.e. for the project fiche. When a project fiche has been accepted in principle by a source of finance, the full application can be elaborated, according to the donor's requirements, which are then known. According to reactions both from bilateral donors, UNDP, REC and others during the EPR review mission, an agreement on such a standard fiche format appears very possible, and all expressed interest in participating.

Once the above is achieved, further improvements in the overall process should be sought, including procedural ones. Such improvements would require a prior relevant study, to which NGOs should be associated, as many investment projects originate from them, and their representation in the present decision processes does not seem to be optimal.

Recommendation 3.1:
There should be a standard format for project descriptions for submission to the Ministry of Environment and Waters when financing of an environmental investment is sought. This format should be prepared by the Ministry of Environment and Waters in cooperation with potential bilateral and multilateral donors. A study should be undertaken on the need for further improvements in the various application processes.

The exchanges between Bulgarian institutions and donors at the yearly donor meetings are very valuable. However, they are insufficient, because donors still lack full, updated information on viable projects after the meetings. The provision of such information on an ongoing basis is important for donors looking for projects to finance, as well as for applicants looking for potential donors. It is in particular proposed (a) to use the Internet to publish project applications (i.e. project fiches), including their principal characteristics, and (b) to establish both more formal and more informal communication between the project recipients and the project managers.

Recommendation 3.2:
Measures that complement the annual donor meetings should be taken. They should ensure efficient and continuous information of donors and applicants about both project and funding opportunities. A detailed study should be undertaken of the current project management routines in the Ministry of Environment and Waters. Any improvement of practices resulting from such a study should be published.

The capacity at MEW to handle the increasing number of projects - latest developments have added ISPA projects to the spectrum - needs to be upgraded in terms of quantity of staff, skill profiles and equipment. The MEW technical sections have all the technical expertise required. The project department staff skills should primarily concentrate on general management, specific project management, financial/economic skills, project organization, project monitoring techniques, contract management, etc. New staff should be selected for such skills, and existing staff should be given relevant training.

Regarding equipment, suitable informatics services need to be available. Efficient computer hardware, databases and software including financial models, project planning tools, etc. would increase capabilities. All standard routines should be computerized, ensuring speed, accuracy, transparency in operations, enabling efficient reporting for different stakeholders, etc. A hotline service via the Internet should be made available to applicants. This should also include distribution of application forms, guidelines for applications, relevant information regarding bilateral donors (e.g. their calls for proposals), etc.

Recommendation 3.3:
The resources of the Ministry of Environment and Waters for project management should be increased, and its staff trained where necessary so that they can acquire the skills needed. They should also be equipped with sufficient information technology to optimize their work.

The routines of project management followed by the MEW should be revised. Especially the following improvements should be made:

- Establishment of written procedures for submission of applications, their receipt and registration at the MEW
- Establishment of a procedure for mandatory acknowledgement to the applicant of the receipt of his application, within two weeks after receipt, including the name of the handling officer and a reference number for the application
- Preparation of clear procedures - in the form of written manuals - for all activities and processes, corresponding to the 'DIS manual' and the 'Manual for procurements and contracting', which are applicable to all EU funded projects.

Regarding the identification of prospective, insufficiently used sources of funding, three directions should be further explored. The first is with bilateral donors. In this respect the implementation of the above recommendations would probably make donors much more forthcoming. Secondly, the debt-for-environment swaps are of course very advantageous for Bulgaria, and it can be expected that initiatives will be taken to increase the number of such agreements in the future.

Thirdly, there is also a local source of funding which does not yet seem to be fully used and which could be encouraged. The source concerned is that of municipal funds.

Today the bulk of municipal income - being taxes and service fees - is collected by the Government and (partly) re-disbursed to the municipalities. The general opinion in municipalities and the public (as regards investments) appears to be that environmental improvements in the environment are the responsibility of the central Government, not of the municipality. Efforts should therefore be made to improve the attitude of municipalities and the public in this regard. One of the possible measures could be to increase the municipal share in the mentioned taxes or fees – notwithstanding the current change in revenue flows as a result of privatization of utilities - if the municipalities are willing to finance more environmental investments themselves.

The law requires disclosure of municipal assets and their independent valuation prior to their sale. However, this procedure does not appear to be publicly trusted. It is recommended, therefore, to draw up an inventory of all municipal assets (hard or soft assets) that are not specifically required for performing the municipal services. The assets should be evaluated at optional cost, when sold under competitive conditions. The inventory should assist the municipalities in proposing an investment plan for the capital which may be realized. This plan should, of course, cover all sectors of municipal responsibilities, not only the environment. The details of the inventory should be made public.

An alternative to the sale of such assets would be their use as bank security for commercial loans. This option could further facilitate co-financing arrangements of environmental investments in municipalities owning such assets. Also, the new possibilities for municipalities (at least the larger among them) to issue bonds may have a positive effect on funding possibilities for environmental investments.

Recommendation 3.4:
Efforts should be made to increase both the willingness and the possibilities of municipalities or regions to finance environmental investments, by:

- *Including financing strategies and means explicitly in the national environmental strategy*
- *Revising the State/municipal ratio for municipal income from environmental payments*
- *Increasing the privatization or sale of municipal assets not required for municipal services*
- *Increasing the use of municipal assets as security for loans contracted by the municipality, particularly as part of co-financing of environmental investments*
- *Further studying the possibilities of issuing municipal bonds.*

See also Recommendation 4.2.

Chapter 4

MANAGEMENT OF AIR POLLUTION FROM STATIONARY INDUSTRIAL SOURCES

4.1 Air emissions, their major sources and air quality

Sectoral emissions

Overall air emissions in recent years are the subject of Table 2.1. Figure 4.1 illustrates the changes that have occurred between 1990 and 1998. Overall, since 1990, the emission of air pollutants has largely decreased. Air emissions from stationary sources are shown in Table 4.1. Industry and automobile transport are the main sources of lead pollution, industry emitting about 55 per cent of it. Industry is also responsible of 95 per cent of cadmium emissions and 76 per cent of mercury emissions. Combustion in manufacturing industries ranks first by far in the production of these heavy metals, be it lead (88 per cent), cadmium (96 per cent) or mercury (76 per cent). Almost a third of cadmium emissions result from the burning of

Table 4.1: Air emissions from stationary industrial sources, by sector, 1998

	Total emission	Sectoral emission				Share of the 3 in the total	Reduction 1990/1998
		Total of the 3 industries	Combustion in energy and transformation industries	Combustion in manufacturing industry	Production processes		
	Thousand tonnes					%	
SO$_x$ (as SO$_2$)	1,251.00	1,163.80	1,031.80	109.50	22.50	93.0	-37.7
NO$_x$ (as NO$_2$)	223.00	121.10	65.60	32.20	23.30	54.3	-38.2
NH$_3$	66.00	15.90	0.00	0.00	15.90	24.1	-54.2
NMVOC	132.00	19.40	0.50	2.20	16.70	14.7	-39.2
CO	650.00	136.50	3.70	89.40	43.40	21.0	-27.0
CH$_4$	553.00	2.20	0.50	1.70	0.80	0.4	-26.9
Lead (Pb) a/	250.78	136.91	4.05	120.91	11.95	54.6	-42.5
Cadmium (Cd) a/	14.87	14.11	0.28	13.58	0.25	94.9	-47.4
Mercury (Hg) a/	4.69	3.58	1.52	1.96	0.11	76.4	-64.5
Polychlorinated biphenyls (PCBs) b/	252.80	54.30	47.50	6.80	0.00	21.5	-2.2
Dioxins & Furans c/	288.43	183.30	119.80	39.40	24.10	63.6	-48.0
Dust (TSP)	233.20	161.80	95.40	63.60	2.80	69.4	..
Polyaromatic hydrocarbons (PAHs) a/	434.02	63.90	35.60	2.80	25.50	14.7	-35.0
Hexachloro-benzene (HCB) b/	76.00	17.00	0.00	0.00	17.00	22.4 d/	-86.0
Pentachloro-phenol (PCP) b/	9.07	4.70	0.00	0.00	4.70	51.8	-81.6

Source: Ministry of Environment and Waters.

Notes:
a/ Expressed in tonnes per year.
b/ Expressed in kg per year. Emissions are calculated according to the mass-balance method based on CORINAIR 1994 Guidelines
c/ Expressed in grams toxic equivalents (Teq) per year.
d/ The rest, i.e. 77.6% are emitted from the treatment and disposal of wastes.

Figure 4.1: Air emissions, 1990-1998

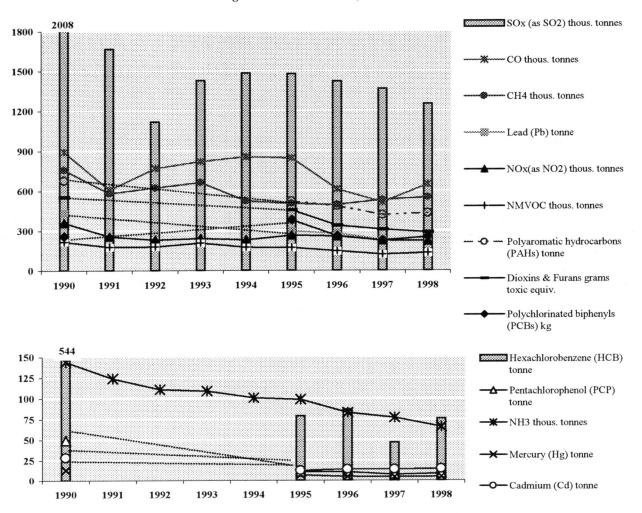

Source: Ministry of Environment and Waters.

liquid fuels in small combustion facilities at local heating stations. Stationary industrial sources generate about 64 per cent of dioxins and furans. Combustion processes are the main source, thermal power plants discharging about 40 per cent of the total.

Ambient air quality and main polluted regions

The quality of ambient air is seriously affected in the vicinity of industrial sites. Table 4.2 includes annual concentrations from some of the most relevant monitoring stations in Bulgaria. The Kremikovtzi station is situated close to the biggest metallurgical plant, Pirdop is near the largest copper smelter, and D. Voden is close to Burgas, the country's biggest petrol refinery.

4.2   Policy objectives and legal framework

Formulation of objectives

The overall policy for air pollution abatement aims at ensuring the country's sustainable development in the field of environmental protection. So far, the following strategies and programmes relevant to air management have been implemented:

- National strategy and action plan on energy development and energy efficiency to the year 2010
- National programme and action plan "Environment and Health"
- National programme on energy efficiency
- National programme on phasing out ozone-depleting substances

Table 4.2: Annual concentration of air pollutants in industrial areas, 1996–1998

mg/m^3

		TSP	Pb	SO_2	NO_2	H_2S	Phenols	NH_3	Cl	HCl	Additional heavy metals	H_2SO_4
Kremikovtsy	1996	0.1470	0.0002	0.0113	0.0761	0.0081	0.0038	n.s	n.s	n.s	n.s	n.s
	1997	0.1456	0.00014	0.0113	0.1074	0.0065	0.0051	n.s	n.s	n.s	n.s	n.s
	1998	..	0.000338	..	..	..		n.s	n.s	n.s	n.s	n.s
Pirdop/REI	1996	0.0811	0.0001	0.033	0.0117	0.0109	n.s	n.s	n.s	n.s	n.s	..
	1997	0.1361	0.00013	0.0287	0.0099	0.0048	n.s	n.s	n.s	n.s	n.s	0.056
	1998	0.2186	0.000136	0.0432	0.0126	0.0057	n.s	n.s	n.s	n.s	n.s	0.3103
D.Voden	1996	0.1780	0.0006	0.1211	0.0141	n.s	n.s	n.s	n.s	n.s	0.0001a/	n.s
	1997	0.1206	0.00034	0.1028	0.0127	n.s	n.s	n.s	n.s	n.s	0.00002 a/	n.s
	1998	0.0986	0.000724	0.0895	0.0145	n.s	n.s	n.s	n.s	n.s	0.00004 a/	n.s
WHO Guidelines		0.06-0.09 mg/m³ b/	0.0005 mg/m³, annual	0.05 mg/m³, annual	0.04 mg/m³, annual							
EU Standards (present)		0.08 mg/m³, annual median value	0.0002 mg/m³, annual	0.08 mg/m³, annual median value if BS≤40 c/	0.2 mg/m³, annual, exceeded not more than 2% time							
		0.13 mg/m³, winter median value		0.12 mg/m³, annual median value if BS≥40								
		0.25 mg/m³, maximum value not to be exceeded more than 3 times annually										
EU Standards (according to IPPC Directive) d/		0.03 mg/m³, annual (50% margin of tolerance)	0.0005 mg/m³, annual (100% margin of tolerance)	0.020 mg/m³, annual and in winter e/	0.04 mg/m³, annual (50% margin of tolerance)							
					0.03 mg/m³, annual as NO and NO₂ to protect vegetation							

Sources: Executive Environmental Agency; WHO Air Quality Guidelines for Europe and EU directive 96/61 on IPPC.

n.s.: Not surveyed

Notes:

a/ CdO

b/ Risk estimates for 24 hours and annual PM10 concentrations.

c/ BS: Black smoke.

d/ IPPC: Integrated Pollution Prevention and Control.

e/ Attainment date: 2 years after entry into force of the IPPC Directive.

- National action plan on climate change.

The Energy Development Strategy of the Republic of Bulgaria to the year 2010 incorporates a number of preventive measures aimed at emission abatement. It brings into play instruments such as fuel and energy prices; measures to increase the proportion of natural gas used in the generation of electric power and thermal energy for industrial purposes, and in the centralized heating system; substitution of low-sulphur solid fuel (0.5 per cent S) in power and heating plants for fuels that are environmentally harmful; the building of eight new 630 MW FGDs in 1999-2010; etc.

The Government prepared and adopted a National Energy Efficiency Programme, which is in full conformity with the basic emissions abatement policy. The Programme relates to almost all sectors, and in particular to energy, industry, regional development and public works. Its implementation, together with other programmes, will require substantial investment.

Priorities for investment were set with reference to the following criteria:

- Risk to human health
- Impact on vulnerable ecosystems
- Fulfilment of international obligations arising from international agreements and treaties
- Location in "hot spot" areas.

On the basis of these criteria, the following priority objectives for investments were determined:

- Limitation of heavy metal emissions from metal industries caused by the use of leaded petrol;
- Limitation of the emission of dust particles from the production of electricity and thermal energy in the metallurgical and other sectors;
- Limitation of the emission of sulphur dioxide and of other noxious gases.

Specifically, the following action is envisaged:

- Construction of desulphurization installations at large combustion facilities; introduction of primary and secondary measures related to nitrogen oxides and rehabilitation of electrostatic precipitators; planning for the desulphurization installations of plants 7 and 8 of the "Maritza-Iztok 2" thermal power station to be operational by 2002;

- Increasing the share of natural gas, and switching to imported coal of low sulphur content through a change in the combustion base and reconstruction of facilities;
- Increasing production of unleaded petrol (0.001 g/l lead), following refinery reconstruction;
- Making provision for the production of diesel fuel with a maximum sulphur content of 0.035 per cent, and of heavy industrial fuel with a content of up to 0.2 per cent by 2004;
- Limiting the sulphur content of diesel to 0.005 per cent, and of heavy industrial fuel to 0.1 per cent after 2005, following refinery reconstruction;
- Reduction of volatile organic compounds emissions during storage and transport of petrol through gradual reconstruction of storage tanks, loading terminals, petrol stations and vehicle petrol tanks by 2010;
- Phased reduction of volatile organic compounds emissions from certain processes, beginning in 2003, involving the reconstruction and modernization of certain industries;
- Reduction of heavy metal and persistent organic pollutant emissions from the energy and industrial sectors by installing filters and absorptive installations during the period 2005-2010;
- Reconstruction and modernization of central heating systems and increasing their use;
- Creation of the necessary infrastructure for increasing the gas supply to household and industrial consumers;
- Reconstruction of existing facilities, and building of new installations in the metal industries to prevent dust, sulphur dioxide and heavy metal emissions.

Targets related to international obligations

The basic priorities of Bulgaria are related to the transposition of the relevant EU legislation, including the application of norms for air quality and industrial air pollution. Specific targets derive from the national priorities and from the obligations implied by ratified global and regional conventions and their protocols pertaining to air pollution. Emission targets are listed in Table 2.3. The table may relate to conventions signed by Bulgaria but not yet ratified and, in such cases, implementation may begin only after ratification.

- During 1999, in accordance with the 1999 Gothenburg Protocol to Abate Acidification, Eutrophication and Ground-level Ozone, new

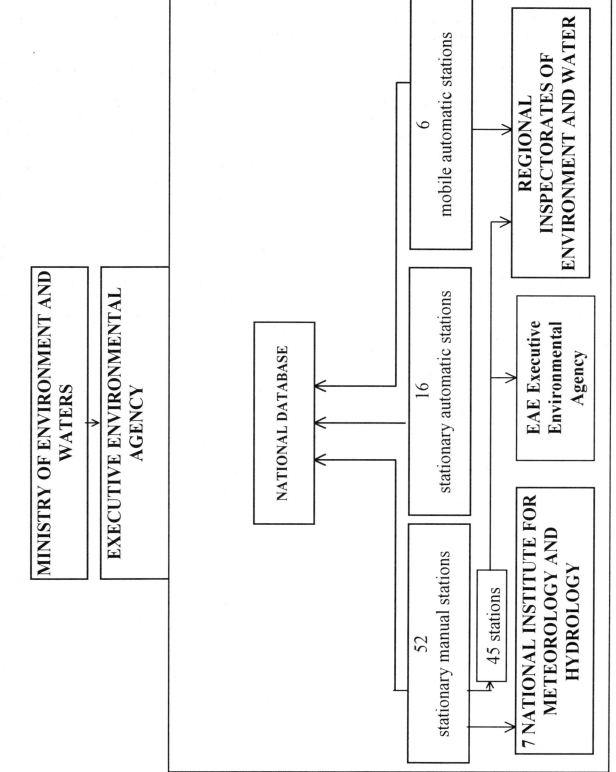

Figure 4.2: Institutions involved in the National Air Quality Monitoring System, 1999

Source: Ministry of Environment and Waters

targets were set for the reduction of emission levels, incorporating all obligations under the previous protocols in force. The Gothenburg Protocol envisages the following reduction of emissions by 2010: for sulphur oxides 57 per cent; for nitrogen oxides 26 per cent; for VOC 15 per cent, and for ammonia 23 per cent.

According to the National Action Plan on Climate Change, which is to be submitted to the Council of Ministers, a number of implementation measures and a scenario for total emission reduction are contemplated. In terms of the scenario, the emissions in 2008 are expected to be 17.5 per cent below, and in 2012 14 per cent below, the base year levels. The aim is to reduce emissions to the levels shown in Table 2.3. The targets set to meet obligations from the Montreal Protocol on HCFCs are also given in Table 2.3.

Legal framework

The Clean Air Act, adopted in 1996, provides for the management of pollution from stationary industrial sources. It establishes the basis required for ambient air quality assessment and management. In principle, emission limit values (ELV) are established for different types of stationary sources. Existing stationary sources may obtain permission from the competent authorities to emit at levels other than those mandatory for new stationary sources. However, in such cases, existing sources are obliged to design and implement programmes to attain conformity with the national standards for new sources. The Act was amended in 2000, to achieve full compliance with the requirements of the EU Framework Directive on Air Quality [96/62/EC], by introducing new AAQ parameters and defining relevant improving programmes and action plans for all non-attainment areas.

The legal instruments relating to air management in general and air management of stationary sources of pollution in particular are listed in Chapter 1. At present, an Act is being prepared on the limitation of VOC emissions, aiming at reduction of the use of solvents in industry. The Act complements the above-mentioned list of available legal instruments and will correspond to European Directive 99/13/EC.

4.3   Institutions and management instruments

Institutional responsibilities

In accordance with the Clean Air Act, the Minister of Environment and Waters (MEW) determines State policy on management of air pollution from stationary industrial sources as part of the overall air pollution abatement policy. The 15 Regional Environmental Inspectorates (REIs under the MEW) and the relevant Municipal Authorities are responsible for the control and management of the relevant activities within their territory, by ensuring the attainment and maintenance of the established air quality standards and emission limit values. The Executive Environmental Agency within the MEW is responsible for the development and maintenance of the National AAQ Monitoring Network and provides methodological guidance to REIs and municipalities.

The Ministry of Health is consulted during the elaboration and adoption of new AAQ standards, and the Ministry of Economy and the State Agency on Energy and Energy Resources, respectively, during the processes of introduction of new emission limit values (for stationary industrial sources).

Economic instruments

The system of charges for exceeding air pollution emission limits was established in 1993. Emission charges and/or taxes are applied according to the quantity of a given pollutant emitted and its characteristics. In controlling the emissions of stationary sources, the 15 Regional Inspectorates of the Ministry of Environment and Waters measure them twice a year. Regional Inspection Directors may levy charges up to 2,000 leva, while for larger sums, the Ministry of Environment and Waters takes the decision. The charges are collected in the NEPF account of the Ministry, but penalized companies may appeal against the charges in court. A Managing Committee, made up of Deputy Ministers from all Ministries, supervises the NEPF, and is chaired by the Minister of Environment and Waters. Expenditure may serve to fund only ecological concerns, as specified in the Regulation on the accumulation, disbursement and control of NEPF funds (SG 75/95).

The 1993 Regulation for the determination and levying of charges for environmental damage and excessive pollution was amended in 1999 (SG 63/99) to address changes in the level of charges. The new rates are included in Table 4.3.

Table 4.3: Charges for the emissions of selected air pollutants

	Leva / kg
Nitrogen oxide emissions from combustion plants	0.12
Sulphur oxide emissions from stationary combustion sources	
- above 500 MW	$0.06 \cdot 10^{3}$
- 100 – 500 MW	$0.6 \cdot 10^{3}$
Lead	45
Cadmium	13.6

Source: Ministry of Environment and Waters.

Charges and taxes, and tax differentiation, are applied also to specific products. Environmental taxes are levied on fuel production and import. In compliance with the amendment to the Clean Air Act (SG 27/00), levied taxes are added to the price of fuel. The National Environment Protection Fund (NEPF) charges the amounts shown in Table 4.4.

Table 4.4: Environmental fuel taxes

	Leva / tonne
Unleaded petrol for light vehicles	24
Diesel fuel	14
Residual oil with sulphur content over 1%	22
Leaded petrol for vehicles:	
- 91 octane petrol	37
- 98 octane petrol	48
Industrial gas oil	13

Source: Ministry of Environment and Waters.

Financial assistance schemes are available to assist enterprises to limit emissions of major air pollutants and have been used to support the introduction of new technologies in the energy, industry and transport sectors. The existing schemes are:

- No-interest loans and cash grants from the National Environment Protection Fund. Financial sources are: pollution charges, taxes, 5 per cent of privatization revenues from the privatization of State enterprises, grants, etc.
- No-interest loans and cash grants from the National Trust EcoFund (SG 63/2995), in which the revenues from the debt-for-environment swaps are accumulated.
- Grants from the EU PHARE programme. The Governments of Denmark, Germany, and the Netherlands, among others, grant significant financial assistance under bilateral agreements for the implementation of joint projects.
- Charge write-offs. By amendment of the Regulation on charges for environmental damage (SG 34/1997), 80 per cent of an emission charge may remain in the company for investing in pollution abatement and achieving permissible emission limit values. An implementation control and supervision procedure was also drafted.
- Value Added Tax (VAT) exemption. By amendment of the Environment Protection Act (SG 62/1998), goods and services imported on International Grant agreements are VAT exempt. An example is the Grant Agreement with the World Bank, amounting to 10.5 million US dollars, for procurement of equipment and technologies for the phasing out of ozone-depleting substances.
- Low-interest loans and accelerated write-off allowances. Such loans, amounting to 80 million US dollars, were received from Japan for the reconstruction of the non-ferrous metals plants in Plovdiv and Eliseina.
- Charge write-offs upon agreement to invest in technological reconstruction and achieving permissible emission limit values for a period not longer than five years are provided for in the Regulation on Temporary Emission Limit Values (SG 51/1998). The technological reconstruction of the non-ferrous metals plant in Pirdop, owned by the Belgian company Union Minière, was negotiated in this way.

A system of tradable permits was established, as for an Environmental Impact Assessment in the industrial or energy sector. The tariff is as follows:

- For a plant of international significance, 0.05 per cent of the project or referential value (the long-term assets, LTA)
- For a plant of national or regional significance, 0.03 per cent of project or LTA value.

Bilateral and multilateral cooperation

The following projects may be mentioned as being of particular relevance to air management:

- Bulgaria participates in the International Joint Programme on the assessment and monitoring of air pollution effects on forests.
- A programme for the approximation of Bulgarian environmental legislation to EU requirements for industrial pollution abatement was implemented with Danish cooperation.
- Bilateral programmes with France, PHARE 98 (ADEME) are being implemented. The subject of cooperation with France concerns the harmonization of air legislation, adaptation requirements of the refineries in Pleven and Burgas to Directives 98/70/EC and 99/32/EC, and of large energy combustion plants in Russe, Varna, Stara Zagora and Bobov Dol to 88/609/EC.
- Bilateral programmes are also being implemented with Germany in 1999, providing support to local air quality management, in accordance with the Ambient Air Quality Framework Directive and its first Daughter Directive.
- In December 1999, a bilateral Memorandum of Understanding was signed between the Bulgarian Ministry of Environment and Waters and the Italian Ministry of Environment which, among other activities relevant to air management, includes joint implementation of greenhouse gas reduction.
- Bulgaria is about to conclude an agreement with The Netherlands on the joint implementation of a programme on greenhouse gas reduction.

Monitoring and data management

Air quality monitoring has been conducted in Bulgaria since 1975. In accordance with the Environmental Protection Act (adopted in 1991 and amended in 1992) the Ministry of Environment and Waters (MEW) is responsible for the monitoring of air quality. One of the main functions of the Executive Environmental Agency (EEA) and the 15 Regional Environmental Inspectorates (REIs) of the MEW, is to collect and process air and water quality data and to provide the interested governmental institutions and the general public with relevant information. For this purpose, EEA and REI have specialized structural units and laboratories. The information obtained through the

air quality monitoring system is used as a basis for setting the national policy and strategy on air quality management as well as for informing decisions on appropriate pollution abatement measures. Another institution involved is the National Institute for Meteorology and Hydrology (NIMH).

A National Air Quality Monitoring System and network is in operation in Bulgaria. The network consist of 68 stationary stations (16 stationary automated and 52 manual stations with sampling and chemical analysis facilities), as well as 6 mobile automated stations. There are 4 "Opsis" systems. The stations are located in 37 settlements all over the country - in urban, residential, high traffic and industrial areas. There is one National Background Station that is part of the GEMS system of UNEP, WMO and UNESCO. It is located on Rojen, one of the highest mountain peaks in Bulgaria.

All manual stations operate in a unified sampling regime and with standardized analytical methods. The sampling frequency is four times a day, five days a week, while the automated stations operate continuously. The basic pollutants quantified are: TSP, Pb, SO_2, NO_2, and H_2S; but for specific industrial activities additional pollutants such as NH_3, phenol, THC, HCl, and Cl_2 are also measured, as well as CO, NO, O_3, and heavy metals Cd and Mn. Automated stations also measure meteorological parameters: wind speed, wind direction, temperature, relative humidity, atmospheric pressure and global radiation. The number of stations that monitor ozone and carbon dioxide is limited because of the lack of automatic monitoring equipment.

In the EEA and REI air quality laboratories, chemical analyses are carried out in accordance with standardized analytical methods. A Quality Handbook, which is periodically updated, is available and measurement accuracy is controlled by setting calibration curves and verification with standard samples, prepared in the laboratory. Comparative assessment of the results of the chemical analyses from different measuring devices is also undertaken. The EEA laboratories are accredited by the Bulgarian Accreditation Body.

Air quality data management is the responsibility of EEA. Raw and aggregated data are stored in local databases in all REIs. After checking for outliers, the data from REIs are entered into the national database maintained by EEA.

Regarding emission inventories, the institutions involved at national and regional or local levels are, respectively, chiefly the MEW, the EEA and REI, and the National Statistical Institute (NSI). Two parallel emission inventory programmes are conducted. The first covers 150 large point sources and is managed by the REI. The second covers nearly 2,000 point sources and is the responsibility of the National Institute of Statistics. The data collected comprise air pollution control facilities and their efficiency, technological and production data, data on fuels used and on fines imposed. For both programmes, the emissions are calculated in accordance with CORINAIR methodology. Data from the emissions inventory are stored at local and national levels, the local databases being maintained at the REI and the NIS. Both institutions provide emission data, updated every year, to the national database in EEA.

EEA and REI conduct measurements of TSP, soot, SO_2, NO_2 emissions and some other specific pollutants to assess compliance with national emission standards.

4.4   Conclusions and recommendations

With the adoption, in January 2000, of the Amendments to the Clean Air Act, the process of transposition of EU Directives in the air quality sector into Bulgarian national legislation is practically complete. At the present time, both the European and the Bulgarian environmental legislation systems are thus harmonized, which represents a considerable achievement on the part of the Bulgarian Ministry, accomplished over the past three years.

The significant changes brought about by the ongoing harmonization of the country's legislation in various fields - not only environmental protection - engenders some implementation and enforcement problems. In practice, it can be difficult to ensure the necessary coordination between the corresponding institutions involved in the process of transposition of EU requirements. As a result, most of the legislation adopted during the past year will also have to be adapted to the country's specific conditions, so as to ensure its effective implementation and enforcement and an adequate degree of synchronization between the different legislative sectors. These adaptations and developmental changes require substantial

resources in both the number of staff dealing with the environmental legislation and the upgrading of their qualifications.

Recommendation 4.1:
The number of staff responsible for the implementation and enforcement of the recently adopted legislation, and the programme for their further qualification in relevant new fields through training programmes, as well as the continuation of the institutional capacity-building process should be reassessed and, if necessary, augmented.

There is an ongoing decrease of air pollution levels, primarily owing to a continuing diminution of industrial and power production, and to the implementation of measures aimed at industrial pollution abatement (including investment in abatement equipment and improvement in the system of collection of taxes and charges). Nevertheless, problems persist in several areas of relevance to air management. Regarding air emissions, the ongoing economic difficulties of the industrial sector cause severe shortages of funds for the purchase and installation of new abatement equipment, or for the rehabilitation and maintenance of existing abatement facilities. Under these circumstances, even the introduction of the best available abatement technologies cannot be expected to achieve particularly dynamic progress. Added problems can easily arise in the strategic policy and social sectors when the use of local fuels, unfortunately of high sulphur content (lignite), is favoured.

The lack of financial resources, together with the need to develop in addition an adequate institutional framework, necessitates the introduction of different transitional provisions (e.g. "gratis periods"), designed to postpone certain specific enforcement requirements of most of the regulatory documents. The main component of this process, however, is still external funding, mainly during the period of implementation of the new legislation. In this situation, the country is increasing efforts to attract more foreign investment funds, but these efforts should be complemented by the elaboration of better domestic financing mechanisms to attract the desired investments. At present, 90 per cent of the financing in this field is covered by the National Environmental Protection Fund (NEPF). This high percentage may in one respect reflect the generally poor economic situation, but it also indicates a relative paucity of domestic funding schemes. It should therefore be envisaged to develop funding schemes that involve foreign and domestic sources of finance at the same time (see also Chapter 3). In addition, the structure of expenditures of the NEPF may have to be reviewed, with a view to finding a better balance between the expenditures for the priorities in all areas of environmental management, including air management.

Recommendation 4.2:
The existing financing mechanisms for air protection investments should be diversified. Co-financing schemes should play a larger role. <u>*See also Recommendation 3.4.*</u>

The existing national air quality monitoring network is well organized, but because of funding difficulties with the maintenance of the monitoring sites, the information available is sometimes only partial. The reason for this is the predominance, in terms of number, of the manual monitoring sites over automatic stations. The manual working stations are generally in operation from Monday to Friday from 9 a.m. to 5 p.m., the quality of the air during the remaining periods of the week not being controlled. However, some industrial activities are operated in a continuous production cycle, partly in response to the differentiation of the price of electricity into peak (morning), normal (afternoon) and night tariffs. The night (including weekend) tariff is the lowest, thereby favouring the maintenance or intensification of some industrial activities during this period, generating emissions that are not well monitored.

The operational and maintenance costs of the monitoring equipment, as well as the continuous training of the air quality specialists require additional funds. Furthermore, funds are also needed for the gradual increase in the share of automatic monitoring.

Recommendation 4.3:
A study should be made of (a) the possibilities to increase industrial self-monitoring, and (b) the measures necessary for future development of the National Air Quality Network. Continuous self-monitoring of large industrial enterprises should be expanded. The study should also identify requirements for new measuring, data transfer and processing equipment in view of the recently adopted new air quality parameters (PAH, benzene, heavy metals and arsenic), and should gradually lead to increased automated air monitoring.

Problems exist with regard to the availability of the meteorological data required to prepare programmes to improve air quality, identification and prioritization of remedial measures, etc. At present, most of these data are owned by the National Institute on Hydrology and Meteorology, which is not in a position to cover the expenses connected with their processing and formatting in a way suitable for air quality modelling. The on-going negotiations between the institutions involved in meteorological data collection, however, are a positive development that should lead to the establishment of a National Meteorological Network. This network would ensure more effective use of the presently available meteorological data for the country's territory.

Recommendation 4.4:
The existing plans for the creation of a National Meteorological Network should be approved and urgently implemented. Such a network should be coordinated with the National Air Quality Network.

Chapter 5

DEVELOPMENT OF SUSTAINABLE WATER MANAGEMENT

5.1 The new framework for water management

The 1997 Strategy for Integrated Water Management

The 1997 Strategy envisages, among other things, water management by catchment area. It is an adaptation of the French experience and is in line with the EU Framework Directive. Water is considered to be a national heritage held in common and managed as a whole under the authority of the MEW, while sectoral uses (for energy purposes, irrigation, domestic drinking-water, etc.) are supervised by sectoral ministries.

In a river basin management scheme management would be extensively decentralized. Basin Councils and Basin Directorates would have wide-ranging authority to implement the national policy set by the government. Permit taxes and water rights would provide some self-financing capacity at the basin level and within a "National Fund for Water Resources". Implementation has been sought in three stages:

- Collecting information, acquiring knowledge and understanding; evolution of institutional responsibilities; drafting legislation and a strategy for water protection and use
- Enforcing the Water Law (regulatory work, creating basin institutions, drafting basin management plans, etc.)
- Establishing the actual working of basin institutions.

A positive accomplishment of the 1997 Strategy was the 1999 Water Act, but because of insufficient means, most of the other tasks it envisaged are either overdue or incomplete. The major weakness, however, is that the Strategy deals essentially with water objects rather than with water systems as a whole.

The 1999 Water Act

The law entered into force in January 2000. The provisions of the Water Act followed the orientations indicated in the 1997 Strategy, i.e.:

Public ownership of - or responsibility for - water, water sites and related main economic systems:

- Management and protection of water objects overseen by the Ministry of Environment and Waters
- Economic water use policies implemented by specific ministries
- Water management to be organized in terms of river basins.

The Water Act envisages water management at three levels: the Council of Ministers, the Ministry of Environment and Waters (MEW) and the Basin Directorates. In addition, the policies for the various uses of water or water ecosystems is determined by sectoral ministries but is expected to comply with the national water policy. When the Water Act entered into force, the MEW asked four of its 15 regional inspectorates to act as temporary substitutes and make provision for the setting up of Basin Directorates. The management by river basin is weaker in the Water Act, however, than as foreseen in the Strategy, as the Basin Directorates are given little financial and regulatory autonomy, and the Basin Councils are not mandated to take final decisions.

National plan and river basin plans

The National Water Economic Plan will be prepared under the guidance of the MEW. It is intended to be the framework for River Basin Management Plans, and for sectoral usage policies. It should be prepared after consultation with other interested ministries, be subjected to public discussion, and reviewed by the National

Consultative Water Council before approval by the Council of Ministers.

The content of the River Basin Management Plans is more or less complete, except for aquatic ecosystem assessment, protection, restoration and use. It is mainly focused on the quantity and quality of water objects and the economy of their uses.

The MEW leads experimental work to prepare a management plan for a sub-basin of the Yantra river, an affluent of the Danube. It is thought that basin management plans should first be prepared on a sub-basin level, where practical local issues can be negotiated. The experience is expected to help the Ministry to assess the complexity and costs of data collection, hydrosystem studies, public information, dialogue and negotiation, all of which will be necessary for the elaboration of a comprehensive basin management plan.

River basin management plans will probably take five to ten years to become available to all Basin Directorates, academic institutions, private engineering companies and local NGOs as required. The Ministry has not yet drafted a plan of action for writing terms of reference, setting priorities and schedules, neither has the staff needed in the Basin Directorates or external organizations yet been assessed nor the costs evaluated.

Permits and control

The spectrum of activities or works that require permits under the new Water Act is quite comprehensive. It includes notably:

- Water regime modifications
- Linear infrastructures encroaching upon water objects
- Extraction and discharge of surface or ground water
- Extraction of sand and ballast
- Use of water objects for recreation, sports, aquaculture.

Depending on the nature or size of the respective objective or activity, the permit is issued by the Council of Ministers, the MEW or the Basin Directorate. However, in all cases, the Basin Directorate will have a major role to play in analysis, negotiating demands and preparing the decision of the mandated body.

The MEW plans to systematically reissue permits for all existing activities. All applications will include an ecological analysis and proposals for remediation, accidental situation management and self-monitoring. The implementation of this plan will eventually fit into the Environment Impact Assessment Procedure and remediation policy of the MEW.

It is obvious that such an authorization scheme will be difficult to implement before some strength and capability is built into the Basin Directorate, and before the Basin Management Plans are drafted and approved. On a river section, where the global effect of all impacts on the whole aquatic ecosystem has to be assessed, individual analysis of impacts is generally irrelevant. Furthermore, the global coherence of individual remediation plans has to be checked against actual quality and quality objectives, to be set by the Basin Management Plan. Before the new authorization and control scheme can function smoothly and effectively, considerable planning and regulatory work is needed. Consequently, the MEW seeks a progressive implementation, starting with provisional permits of three years' duration, which can be revised once Basin Management Plans are available. Permits may require a scheduled reduction of impacts, associated with an investment plan.

Financial incentives

The Water Act defines principles for economic stimulation of rational use, protection and restoration of water and water objects. Water prices are set at levels covering the full cost of services, the polluter-pays principle is to be implemented, and payments are a function of the quantity used or the pollution loads generated. As an incentive to water savings, water supply companies and associations cannot charge users the cost of water losses exceeding 25 per cent of the water abstracted.

The law is quite clear about administrative fees, fines for violating the law, and remedies for damage to water objects. The amount of fees to be paid will be established by the Basin Directorates, and collected by the National Environmental Protection Fund. The tariff for fees are either determined by the law, or fixed by the Council of Ministers. It is not entirely clear, how the polluter-pays principle is implemented in terms of the fees for water use. To induce rational use of water

Figure 5.1: Quality of Surface Waters in Bulgaria, 1996-1998

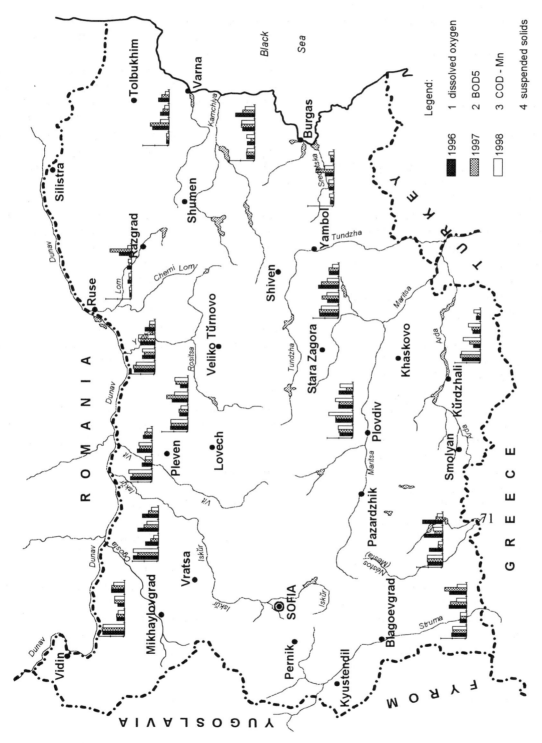

bodies, fees should include the external costs of user activities, and this would call for further legislative and regulatory development.

The National Environmental Protection Fund may allocate subsidies or loans to water users for water protection investment. Basin Directorates have no direct control over financial incentive schemes that might be applied, this being a major limitation to basin management.

5.2   Hydrosystem monitoring

Hydrological monitoring

Hydrological monitoring is managed and operated by the National Institute of Meteorology and Hydrology, a branch of the Academy of Science. Its programmes and budget are initially prepared by a scientific advisory council, before being approved by the president of the Academy. The programme is not easily suited to other users' needs for hydrological information (administrations responsible for the environment, hydro-electricity, flood protection, irrigation, etc.).

The Institute operates 209 stations on rivers (132 with limnigraphs) and 461 for ground water monitoring (328 wells and 133 springs). The technical quality of river gauging, level measurement, and discharge evaluation is excellent, but the equipment is rather old (20 years or more) and inefficient. All data for the year are available in April of the following year. Four automatic real-time telemetric stations, integrated into the international Metrokos Project and financed by the World Bank, are operated by the Institute. The staffing and the number of gauging stations is half of what it was in 1989. This has led to a serious lack of information about the country.

Data management, data analysis and publication are rather scant. Paper publications are delayed, computerized data and standard hydrological analysis are not publicly available, and are sold by the Institute in an effort to acquire financial resources. General statistical indicators for the stations are not available. Correction for hydro-electricity operations and large abstractions are not performed on a routine basis.

Physico-chemical monitoring

The Executive Environmental Agency is in charge of chemical monitoring of the surface and underground water resources. This monitoring is not fully co-ordinated with the hydrological monitoring. The Executive Agency has its own discharge measurement teams for the quality monitoring stations.

For surface waters, a new network of 254 stations that comply with the Eurowater standard has been in operation since July 1997. Since 1 January 2000, 111 of the stations have been integrated into the Euronetwork of the EU, managed by the WRC in England. No linkage scheme was designed using data from the previous network that had provided data since 1976. However, the quality of sampling and analysis is satisfactory, although relatively inefficient due to insufficient equipment and management.

Data management, analysis and publishing need extensive improvement to transform the raw data into information suitable for water quality assessment, policy planning and control, for the emerging Basin Directorates.

There is no organized monitoring of organic or metallic toxic substances in sediments or biological accumulators (aquatic plants or fish). The trophic status of rivers and lakes is not monitored.

Simple groundwater quality parameters are monitored at about 250 stations. For financial reasons, most of them are located at drinking water abstraction points, a practice that does not permit satisfactory monitoring of the general quality of groundwater.

Hydro-biological monitoring

Hydro-biological monitoring has been carried out since 1992, using a standard bioindex method. It is a rather detailed monitoring, performed in river basins every six years or so. A useful complement to the physico-chemical monitoring could be obtained, if yearly evaluations would be carried out for a significant proportion of the stations, appropriately distributed over the whole river network.

Ecosystem monitoring

Aquatic ecosystems are not monitored on an organized basis with standard protocols. The most important national Ramsar Convention wetland is monitored by academic institutes and NGOs, generally in connection with the MEW and some kind of technical and financial agreement.

Analytical laboratories

The Executive Environmental Agency manages a main laboratory in its Sofia facility, and regional laboratories in the Regional Environmental Inspectorates. The production of data from physico-chemical monitoring is of satisfactory quality, but the lack of automated laboratory instruments is a limitation on the efficiency of the operation. The laboratories do not appear to be ready to confront a large increase in quantity or a change in the type of analysis - a capacity that will be needed in the future. The evolution of the situation in the direction of few independent laboratories, capable of handling large volumes of data, and working with increased efficiency and effectiveness, under a certification scheme managed by the Executive Environmental Agency, and charging real costs to any user, is a likely perspective.

Monitoring of water resources: uses and pressures

The most important water abstracts are available in terms of yearly volumes. The data are collected on forms, which are sent both to the statistical agency and the Executive Environmental Agency. There are no specific data covering the dry season, when minimum runoff in rivers may be insufficient. Detailed data on the modification of water regimes by dams and reservoirs are kept by their operators, but no central collection of such data takes place. This could well be difficult, owing to the absence of a common monitoring protocol.

Urban and industrial discharges are monitored through forms filled in annually by the regional water companies and the 1,070 industrial facilities, reporting on the volumes treated (mechanically and biologically) and discharged. Similar but different forms have to be filled in for the national statistical agency and for the Executive Environmental Agency. For control purposes, occasional sampling and analysis of discharged water is carried out. No information is available about industries discharging into urban sewage networks.

Due to the lack of detailed monitoring of the treatment processes, self-monitoring of the discharging activity, and sufficient control analysis, it is not possible to estimate yearly or seasonal pollution loads discharged into rivers. It is hoped that in a not too distant future, the Water Act will provide for better monitoring of discharged pollution loads under the authority of the Basin Directorates.

Little is known about effluent management by important cattle breeding farms, and whether slurry and manure are used as fertilizer or discharged. No data is available for nitrate or pesticide discharges into groundwaters from large intensive or irrigated cropping.

5.3   Drinking-water   and   waste-water treatment

General organization

The Water Act of 1999 does not provide unequivocal guidance concerning the ownership of facilities, nor determine the legal responsibility for providing drinking water and sewerage. At the national level, the Ministry of Regional Development and Public Works has the global responsibility for drinking-water supply. The Ministry of Health is in charge of quality control of drinking water. Until 1999, most facilities were owned and operated by publicly owned companies at the district level. There were 22 such companies. Since 1999, 49 per cent of the ownership of those water and sewerage companies has been transferred to municipalities. The Sofia water and sewerage company was a municipal property and partially privatized in 1999.

Treatment facilities

It is generally acknowledged that most drinking-water and sewerage facilities in Bulgaria are in poor condition, due to faulty design and building, and lack of maintenance and ineffective operation as a consequence of the decline of the economic situation in the past decade. Average leakage in the drinking-water distribution network is more than 50 per cent. External pollution of distributed water is frequent. Most of the network is built from asbestos-cement pipes and needs replacement.

Policy

The current fundamental objective in medium- and long-term planning for investment, maintenance operations and water prices, is to attain financial equilibrium without permanent public subsidies. The investments are planned to meet EU standards. Delegation of the management of facilities is pursued as a means to facilitate financing and technology transfer, as well as providing for better operations and water price collection.

The Sofia facilities, apart from the waste-water treatment plants, have been under concession since

1999. Tenders for concessions for the municipality of Varna, and for Dobrich and Shumen, two other municipalities nearby, are expected by the end of the year 2000. In the years to come, the Ministry of Regional Development expects privatization to increase considerably.

Water price development scenario

The average price paid by domestic users for drinking water is 0.55 leva per cubic metre (in a range of 0.30-1.20 leva), and the price for sewerage 0.15 leva (range of 0.10 - 0.20 leva). This price level represents a two- to fourfold increase since 1989, in a move to substitute user payments for subsidies. Due to declining income and the deficient system of collection of payments due, a significant number of individual users do not pay, but no global data were available at the time of the EPR Review Mission. Industries which are traditionally used to very low water prices are heavy users of drinking water, and under the present degraded economic conditions, many of them cannot pay their higher priced bills.

Even taking into account the low level of wages and potential improvement in efficient water use, still higher relative water prices will be required in the future to meet EU standards for drinking water and waste-water treatment. An average price of 2 leva per m³ would be a minimum. This is clearly unacceptable within the next ten years for social and economic reasons. It is clear that an effective growth of revenues from drinking-water sales will take years to materialize, and will be linked to economic recovery. It is therefore necessary, when planning long-term investment, to recognize that improvements of this type of income will be slow and, in the meantime, to organize some form of public funding.

Planning for the renewal of facilities

Water companies do not develop a comprehensive long-term investment plan. Detailed knowledge or estimates of discharged pollution loads is not yet available, choices about the separation of sewerage for rainwater and waste water have not been made, the scheduling of repairs or reconstruction of sewerage networks has not been established, choices about storm water management before discharge are not clear, control over industrial discharges into urban sewerage networks is not effective, actual waste water levels are unknown and schedules of treatment (BOD and later nutrient) cannot be implemented, the disposal of treatment

sludge requires integrated, interdependent pre-engineering studies, and financial evaluations and global scheduling are not yet available.

In 1999, in response to EU requirements, MEW prepared a national programme for priority construction of urban waste-water treatment plants for populated areas with over 10,000 Eq. inhabitants. The programme has been approved by the Council of Ministers.

There are plans for developing the use of domestic waste-water treatment sludge as fertilizer as an alternative to landfill dumping. The implementation of such a plan, if dangerous hazards to soils in terms of pollution by toxic elements are to be avoided, would presuppose the existence of substantial, complex controls of industrial discharges in most important cities. Landfilling of sludge, accompanied by control and proper management or treatment of lixiviated waters, might thus have to be favoured in most cases for quite a few years.

Delegated management and restructuring of water companies

The existence of large water companies at the district level is a real advantage, for both technical and economic reasons. In this respect, the Bulgarian situation is similar to that of the United Kingdom. It is easier to optimize the use of production factors at the regional level, as well as to negotiate and control sub-contracts. Unfortunately, institutional factors seem to favour the disaggregation of water companies into smaller entities at the municipal level, as follows:

• The Water Act does not prescribe the setting up of institutional associations of municipalities at the district level to take responsibility for drinking-water supply and sewerage. Therefore, there is no single legal authority entitled to negotiate and control a global concession on behalf of all the interested municipalities and the government.

• Bulgarian law has no provision for public subsidies to private companies. Since national and international financing is expected for waste-water treatment plants, this part of a company's water facilities will frequently be separated for later privatization. This was the case in the 1999 concession of the Sofia facilities.

• Representatives of municipalities may not yet have sufficient understanding of the issues related to the delegation of public services or facilities. This makes it difficult for them to agree on a common policy. Local interests, and private operators of drinking water and sewerage companies, have a natural tendency to try to retain the most profitable parts of water facilities.

Protection of drinking-water resources

Most drinking water is abstracted from groundwater, and a lesser part (as for Sofia) from multi-purpose artificial reservoirs. Villages, especially in mountainous areas, draw drinking water from a large number of small springs, but this does not account for a large part of the population. Quality monitoring managed by the National Centre for Hygiene, Medical Ecology and Nutrition shows a 20 per cent rate of non-conformity to the national standards (which are in line with EU standards). But most of the non-conformity is not viewed as serious by the Ministry of Health.

Along with the bad condition of distribution networks, the bad quality of water objects and the insufficient treatment of raw water are the major causes of non-conformity. Therefore, the protection of resources from industrial, agricultural or domestic pollution is an important problem, requiring future resolution. Alluvial ground waters are polluted through soil pollution from industry or agriculture, and the protection at the point of abstraction is too local to be effective in large feeding areas. Eutrophication of reservoirs is frequently a source of difficulty in customary treatment processes.

A significant proportion of drinking water from alluvial reservoirs is close to the 50 mg/l standard for nitrates. This is not a public health priority for the Ministry of Health, but it could become a future issue for the agricultural policy in large irrigated plains, along with the presence of agrochemicals not yet monitored.

5.4 Hydroelectric and irrigation dams and reservoirs

The total reservoir volume is 5,000 million cubic metres. This volume is 15 to 30 per cent of the natural runoff of Bulgarian rivers. Three million cubic metres belong to the dams and cascades of the national electric company, which operates 43 dams, 6,171 km of derivations and 500 abstraction sites. A new big dam is under construction on the Arda river, in cooperation with Turkey, and there is

an important project to complete the derivations and abstractions scheme for the hydroelectric complex in the southern mountains.

This hydraulic infrastructure has a considerable impact on the water regime and, subsequently, on various aspects of the aquatic ecosystem in the reservoir lakes and downstream. It affects the temperature and quality of water flowing from the reservoirs, can cause insufficient runoff in derived segments or upstream rivers, modification of seasonal variability, a huge daily variation of runoff, and subject biodiversity to stress. The potential impact of the discharge of sludge accumulated behind the dams when they require emptying for control or maintenance, has not yet been provided for. The hope that no emptying will ever be necessary seems optimistic.

A process of privatization and concessions should be considered in the next few years for hydroelectricity facilities and, in the longer term, for irrigation reservoirs and main supply networks. An extended and detailed Environmental Impact Assessment of hydraulic equipment and operations would then be necessary, at least to guide the planning of new investments and the terms of future concession or privatization contracts. Such assessment will certainly show the environmental and economic interest of some remediation work to be incorporated in the contracts and scheduled within the next 20 or 30 years.

5.5 Irrigation and drainage

In the years 1950 to 1989, Bulgaria set up huge agro-engineering drainage and irrigation works. They were built and managed by the national irrigation company, whose staff now comprises 2,600 (at the head office in Sofia and 22 regional branches). This company has an excellent technical capacity with regard to agro-hydraulic issues, and exports its know-how to a number of other countries.

The maximum extension of irrigation was reached in 1989, with 800,000 ha. This surface corresponds to 20 per cent of arable cropland in Bulgaria, and most of the flat alluvial plains. Drainage and irrigation are associated with 80 million cubic metres of water reserves in 200 dams, and the necessary network of mains and collectors, mostly gravitational. The national irrigation company manages 3,000 km of dikes for flood protection. Drainage water is pumped from the collectors into the rivers. Irrigation water is pumped from the reservoirs and, mostly, from rivers (eventually re-fed from the large multi-purpose reservoirs managed by the hydro-electricity company). The main crops grown are corn, rice, vegetables, and fruit.

The yearly water use for irrigation ranges from 1,000 to 5,000 cubic metres per hectare, according to climate and crop. The total irrigation needs for a 1/5 frequency dry year could reach 2,500 million cubic metres, i.e. most of the natural runoff during the irrigation season. The impacts of irrigation and drainage on river ecosystems and on alluvial groundwater quality are not being comprehensively assessed.

Since 1989, this infrastructure, which cannot be adequately maintained, is degenerating rapidly. Farmers are reluctant to pay for irrigation water (rates are 0.05 leva for gravity adduction and 0.30 leva for pressure water), and the needs are decreasing along with demand for and production of agricultural goods. The income of the irrigation company is far from being sufficient to finance the necessary maintenance and repair work. The land redistribution programme disrupted the farmers' organization necessary for the management of the irrigation and drainage facilities. The irrigated surface therefore shrank by 28 per cent to 580,000 ha. The national irrigation company expects and is planning for a long-term technical-economic equilibrium at 400,000 ha of irrigated land.

Plans are being prepared for major repairs and restructuring of the network at this reduced scale. The technical and financial feasibility of a two-step programme (for implementation in 2000-2025 and 2025-2050, respectively) is being examined together with the World Bank, whose financing is expected. Complementary schemes are being prepared to organize farmers into local irrigation associations, responsible for end-of-line hydraulic networks and crop selection. The main infrastructures could be privatized by river basin management in a few years. The objective is to revive agricultural production, increase farmers' income, and bring the Bulgarian agro-hydraulic heritage to economic efficiency. The protection or remediation of aquatic ecosystems is not yet a major concern. Consequently, this area offers opportunities for the development of further project objectives.

5.6   Water pollution from waste management

Lixiviated or accidental pollution from waste deposits or tailing ponds are a major hazard to surface and groundwater in Bulgaria, as well as to aquatic ecosystems. A precise assessment and monitoring of this hazard for effects of radioactive tailings of the closed uranium industry is being undertaken, and a remediation plan is being developed. Similar action is lacking for groundwater and river pollution from other industrial and mining waste deposits. Heavy metal pollution in river sediments appears to be rather widespread, but is neither appropriately surveyed nor monitored. Waste sites are not considered to be pollution discharges to rivers and groundwaters but in fact should be regulated as such.

New mining concessions (for gold ore in particular) are potentially hazardous to rivers and require regulation for careful (and costly) waste management.

5.7   Aquatic ecosystems

Systematic surveys of river and riverside ecosystems are in general lacking, or scant. In mountains, river ecosystems downstream of mining waste dumps and hydro-electric works are probably seriously affected. The standard arrangement for rivers flowing through plains (dykes and drainage of riparian space) destroyed their natural ecology leading to poor biodiversity.

Valuable knowledge of major wetlands (notably in the Danube and the Black Sea areas) was derived from their ornithological interest and the Ramsar Convention. Their biodiversity is extremely rich (in terms of birds, fish, mammals, insects, plants, etc.). Large areas along the Danube river were destroyed, however, by agro-engineering works. A partial revivification of such areas has been left for the future.

Most of the Bulgarian wetlands of major interest have been impacted by industrial pollution, civil engineering works modifying the water regime, or destroying habitats. A plan for remedial action was drafted for the MEW, but its enforcement depends on strong political will and finances which are not yet clearly identified and available.

5.8   Conclusions and recommendations

Despite the fact that there has been no sign of improvement in river water quality since the mid-nineties, a very positive development is the growing consciousness and understanding of the unsatisfactory situation and the building of a suitable institutional framework to overcome the difficulties. The EU accession goal gives a strong impulse to Bulgarian water policy. But in some respect this policy appears imperfectly grounded in reality and needs. A clear strategy with the financial and human capability to implement it has still to be set.

The 1999 Water Act of Bulgaria is an excellent framework for the development of sustainable water management. Its implementation will be long, difficult and expensive, more than is usually expected in the country, and the actual building of this solid foundation for sustainable water management should be the highest priority. Building up the monitoring network and the basin institutions call for detailed action plans, funded and controlled by the Water Directorate of the MEW, and should be implemented by the future River Basin Directorates.

Recommendation 5.1:
Based on the Water Act of 1999, detailed action plans should be drafted and implemented for the installation of a related monitoring network and the creation of the necessary basin institutions. The implementation of such plans should be designated a priority for international funding. The monitoring system should become part of a modern system of data collection, analysis and dissemination to all user groups.

Substantial time, effort and financing are required to improve the monitoring, as well as the knowledge and understanding of water ecosystems. The MEW should rapidly draft short- and long-term plans of action and allocate a substantial share of available public finances to their implementation. It is suggested that the implementation of such plans should also become a priority for international financing.

The national water monitoring system should be extended. Particularly required are more frequent bio-index measurements, monitoring of toxic elements in sediments and biological integrators, and measurement of the geomorphology and ecology of water systems. The constitution of a few independent laboratories for analysis of monitoring

samples should be planned and facilitated. Such labs should be allowed to work for any public or private organization. Large sized laboratories, the prescription of common sampling and analysis protocols, and a certification procedure could induce efficiency and quality.

The data production function of the National Institute of Meteorology and Hydrology should be integrated into the national water monitoring system and achieve some independence from the Academy of Science. The main users of such data (academia; administrations dealing with the environment, agriculture, energy, and regional development; NGOs and others) should be associated with the development of the objectives for the network.

The Executive Environmental Agency should develop more standard data analysis and presentations using raw data from monitoring. This is necessary to nourish the decision, planning and control processes effectively. A number of such quality assessment tools are available in the EU, defining quality classes for the main uses of water, its sites, and the way to compute the actual quality class from the raw data.

The practical implementation of most monitoring, data management and analysis, quality assessment, public data and information dissemination should be done by the Basin Directorates, under the authority of and following protocols issued by the Executive Environmental Agency. The Agency should be in charge of national aggregation, synthesis, and information. It is a general recommendation that more value can be expected from monitored data nationwide when they are publicly and easily available at low cost. Such diffusion has now been facilitated by Internet technologies.

River surveys are urgently needed in Bulgaria for relevant river basin planning, enabling the identification of issues as well as their analysis. They should be managed by the Basin Directorates under the authority and guidelines of the MEW. Sufficient funding should be allocated as soon as possible. As in the case of monitoring, the surveys should become a priority for domestic and international financing. The carrying out of the surveys, following an appropriate process of tendering, can provide an opportunity to strengthen the ability to conduct such studies among Basin Directorates, NGOs, academic institutions and private engineering companies. It is also recommended that over the next five to ten years mixed Bulgarian/EU member-country teams be favoured as a vector for technological transfer.

More attention should be given to the physical and hydrobiological aspects of water systems, which are currently only considered as a natural infrastructure and major producer of quantitatively regulated water of good quality. Training, communication, testing for river basin management plans, and the permit process in both the Basin Councils and Basin Directorates will progressively build efficient processes.

Recommendation 5.2:
The future River Basin Directorates should, as a matter of priority, undertake river basin surveys and identify and analyse issues for corresponding basin planning. Furthermore, in their work, they should give special attention to the physical and hydrobiological aspects of water systems. The task necessitates the presence of adequate expertise in the future Councils and Directorates.

The perspective for privatization of hydro-power generation, and the need for extensive restructuring, repair and maintenance of the irrigation system should provide a real opportunity for a better integration of those major impacts on the hydrosystem. Extensive Environmental Impact Assessment of the facilities and their operations are needed. They should, among other effects, cover the ecological consequences of modified runoff regimes and water quality, and the pollution of ground and surface water by intensive irrigated agriculture. Long-term schedules for remedial action should be included in the privatization deals and in the restructuring of irrigation facilities.

The renaturation of some important drained wetlands along the Danube river is a priority of the national plan for restoring and protecting wetlands. Further, irrigation restructuring is an opportunity to study and organize a real protection of groundwater resources by inducing permanent vegetation, low yield high quality agricultural practices on large areas, feeding the groundwater abstraction stations. It is also an opportunity to create "green corridors" some 50 to 100 metres wide along rivers in irrigated plains and to restore some natural functions of surface and underground aquatic ecosystems.

Recommendation 5.3:
The generation of hydro-electricity, as well as irrigation schemes, should be better integrated into

hydrosystem management efforts. The tool of Environmental Impact Assessment should be used extensively in this regard. Long-term remediation programmes should be part of privatization contracts, particularly for irrigation schemes. Needs derived from the declared objectives of wetland restoration and of general nature management should be taken into account.

The integrity of regional water companies is a powerful advantage, which should be strengthened through comprehensive long-term integrated planning of action and investment. In all respects, regional water companies have opportunities for economic and technical economies of scale and efficient cooperation between neighbouring municipalities. It is therefore recommended that disaggregation of regional water companies be avoided. This would call for some regulatory and legislative adjustments:

- The association of municipalities and the State within legal authorities for the purpose of organizing drinking-water supply and waste-water sewerage and treatment should be introduced into the legal system. Corresponding institutional bodies should have the right to delegate and control these functions after their possible privatization or concession.
- Subsidization of private companies in charge of delegated management of a regional water company should become a legal possibility.

The Ministry of Regional Development and Public Works and the MEW should develop guidelines for the urban water management delegation process and respective contracts, by agreeing on accounting rules, economic and quality auditing, price evolution, negotiation rules, investments programmes, required public financing, and other relevant conditions. Some transfer of experience could be obtained from EU countries, particularly the United Kingdom, where an elaborate control scheme is operated for regional companies.

Recommendation 5.4:
Modifications should be made in regulatory and legislative rules in order to maintain the operation of regional water companies. The Ministries of Regional Development and Public Works and of Environment and Waters could enhance the delegation of urban water management to regional companies through the joint development of appropriate guidelines. The necessary control scheme could be based on relevant practices in European Union member countries.

Sound integrated long-term plans are necessary to underlie and circumscribe proper investment or delegation. Complete and precise pre-engineering studies for all water companies, undertaken by independent engineering firms, could help to fill this gap. It could be a priority for international funding. Financing, tender and supervision of such studies should be managed by the regional water companies, under close control by the municipalities, the MRDPW and the MEW. The studies would contain:

- An assessment and analysis of the actual state of facilities
- A schedule for reaching goals for adequate drinking water supply, for quality of water discharges, for availability and protection of water objects, for storm water and for sludge management
- A long-term global investment plan (including broad technical specifications, costs, revenues, and funding of facilities)

Recommendation 5.5:
Pre-engineering studies by independent engineering firms should be undertaken for all water companies, under the joint control of the Ministry of Regional Development and Public Works, the Ministry of Environment and Waters, and the Municipalities concerned, possibly financed from international sources.

More focus on all components of aquatic ecosystems (river beds and embankments, wetlands and riversides) is needed. The institutional framework in Bulgaria focuses on water quantity, quality and economic uses, but does not clearly support an integrated apprehension of water systems in the broad sense (quantity and quality of water *as well as* the aquatic ecosystems and the physical milieu where water runs). In this sense,

the water systems are, among other benefits, the most effective infrastructure for water quality and quantity and should be known, protected and managed as such.

The privatization policy and various planning processes can be a real opportunity for better sustainable management of water systems, but this is not fully recognized and accounted for.

The consistency of water plans with the national or regional user plans calls for explicit guidelines, including assessment and arbitration procedures. Such general hydrosystem protection guidelines for water usage plans should be prepared under the responsibility of the ministries responsible for regional development, agriculture, and energy. They should be drafted in agreement with the MEW and the Ministry of Health and then be approved by the Council of Ministers. They should stipulate the inclusion of explicit measures for hydrosystem protection in the national and local plans by the aforementioned ministries, when using or impacting water and aquatic ecosystems. The measures should be subject to approval by the MEW.

Recommendation 5.6:
The necessary guidelines ensuring consistency between water plans and water use requirements at national and regional level should be developed in cooperation between the ministries concerned and should include explicit measures for aquatic ecosystem protection.

Recommendation 5.7:
The reduction of excessive water use, as well as of losses of water in distribution, should remain priorities for water management. A policy regarding the long-term development of water prices should become an instrument for the achievement of these goals.

Chapter 6

DEVELOPMENT OF RELIABLE WASTE STATISTICS

6.1 Waste statistics in relation to waste policy and management

General considerations

Waste statistics primarily try to respond to information requirements appearing in waste management and waste policy. The collection, compilation and dissemination of statistics need to be adapted to the major waste policy targets and the different activities, on which statistical waste information is needed. Each subject area may need special consideration in statistical production. The main areas for waste statistics required are avoidance of waste, generation of waste, recycling, treatment, transport and disposal of waste.

In general, official waste statistics are confronted with the demand to show the flow of wastes from the point of generation to the final destination including the processes described below. The quantities of waste should be subdivided in a way sufficient for a large number of different users of the statistics. This implies their subdivision by type of waste and/or activity generating waste. However, they should not be specified with respect to their suitability for recycling or environmentally friendly disposal, or other interested qualifications. The statistical system must also be internally coherent, a requirement that has substantial repercussions on the organization of the specialized statistics for different sectors – and the relationships of waste statistics with other parts of the statistical system of a country.

Avoidance of waste

In the hierarchy of political targets for waste management, the avoidance of waste holds the top position. From a systematic point, one has to distinguish between prevention of waste generation and reduction of such generation. In practice, prevention means that a product or a substance within a product are eliminated, resulting in lesser or different waste. The administrative tool reaching this target could be the banning of production.

Reduction of the quantity of waste generation, on the other hand, or of the presence of one pollutant in a composite waste, may result from a change in the production process caused by independent management decision or - when households are concerned – from voluntary cancelling the use of a product causing disposal problems.

Reuse of material and products is another form of avoiding waste. Examples are multiple use of packaging, clothes, furniture or toys (sold in second-hand shops), spare parts for equipment, or internal circuits of lubricating oils. The borderline between reuse and recycling is blurred. In general, reuse is a suitable topic for statistical reporting, provided that a definition is available that clearly distinguishes this type of material from primary material as well as from waste.

Generation of waste

The quantities of anthropogenic waste are rising steadily. This applies to the main types of waste in terms of volume or weight, i.e. production and consumption waste. Waste originating in pollution abatement must be regarded as a third source of waste generation, as the measures for purification of ambient air, water and soil lead to waste like filter dust or sludges.

The information about generated waste are the basic data which determine the measures taken in the management of waste treatment and disposal. The primary prerequisite is completeness of information. In practice, this means that all sectors of the economy and the private households must be included in the statistical account, and that all quantities of generated waste have to be considered.

Structuring the activities that generate waste by their main economic activity is quite common. This information gains importance when the economic impact and social consequences of environmental regulations are discussed. A sound answer to the question of what is reasonable needs very detailed information. However, such data in fine breakdown will normally have to be obtained through special analysis, using many different sources, rather than from statistics alone that are routinely collected. The reason is that it is relatively expensive to collect data from generators in a very detailed breakdown by activity, and to combine them with detailed data on waste. A large part of the demand for information can normally be satisfied by applying an aggregated list of economic activities, so that it would be uneconomical to collect statistics routinely in their most detailed form.

As indicated above, a distinction between primary waste (from production and consumption processes) and secondary waste (generated in waste treatment installations), and in addition between non-hazardous and hazardous is essential. The types of waste are collected from different activity units, requiring each time tailor-made collection techniques. Furthermore, the storage and analysis of the basic data are different, as are the waste management context, in which they are needed.

A main concern for statistical work is a waste list or catalogue, which should be obligatory for waste management at all levels, or accepted nationwide. Reporting of waste data, even on the basis of an agreed waste list is in practice never complete, and the dealing with reporting deficiencies is perhaps the major methodological challenge for waste statisticians. Solutions to the problem vary between different respondents or reporting institutions. For example, experience shows that some parts of the economy like private households and many enterprises from the tertiary sector provide only limited data about the quantities and types of waste they produce. Consequently, waste lists for use in the context of waste generation by private households and service enterprises should be shorter, i.e. show a higher degree of aggregation.

Recycling

Another target of waste management and policy is to obtain a high share of recycled waste. Obviously, recycling must be practicable in a technical sense, surplus costs should be reasonable compared with other disposal methods, and finally there must exist a market for the recovered material or energy.

Recycling is a primary task of the waste generators, mostly industrial plants. It can be realized on-site or by external operators. One distinguishes between material-oriented and energy-oriented recycling. The first group always needs some specific installation to recover useable raw materials from

the waste. Several techniques are known and applied, so that it is desirable to report data for each type of material. Energy-oriented recycling means combustion of waste. The intention is to use the heat content directly or after transformation into e.g. electricity. The installations are specialized (i.e. incineration plant with energy recovery) or normal furnaces, in which larger quantities of waste are burnt regularly.

The most economical point at which statistical base data should be collected are the recycling installations.

Treatment

A third set of statistical information should deal with waste treatment. The activities resumed in this group are destined to destroy the pollutants contained in waste or to immobilize them. The treatment processes shall meet some demands like

- avoiding substantial quantities of gaseous emissions
- preventing uncontrolled and unwanted chemical or other reactions of waste
- avoiding or minimizing the appearance of pollutants in leachate.

There are biological, chemico-physical and thermal methods in operation. The results of treatment are secondary wastes. Here again, the obvious primary target for statistical enquiry is the treatment installation.

Final disposal

The landfill site plays an important role for the final disposal of waste and will hold this position in the near future. In spite of increasing efforts for recycling, wastes will remain that must be finally stored.

In landfills in which biodegradable wastes are disposed, e.g. traditional household waste or sludge sites, uncontrolled physical, chemical and, above all, biological processes take place, resulting in unpredictable emissions in the leachate or in gas produced on or emitted from the site. Major management concerns are connected with this circumstance. The potential danger of a landfill site to human health or the environment can only be documented by monitoring with chemical and physical methods, i.e. cannot be the role of statistics. Statistics should be confined to reporting some technical features of the sites, which are generally supportive of the management measures taken to reduce risks.

6.2 Waste statistics in Bulgaria

Legal basis

In conjunction with the Bulgarian statistical law, waste statistics can be ordered by the Council of Ministers. Certain changes in statistical characteristics and other methodological parts of a survey may be realized within the responsibility of the National Statistical Institute (NSI). As a result, the legal basis provides a relatively high degree of flexibility to the NSI to react on changes in waste legislation.

Data collection and terminology

Since 1980, the NSI conducts two yearly surveys on waste. In these surveys the term "waste" was defined as residuals which the generator wants to get rid of. Material recycled or reused at the place of generation was excluded. The term "municipal waste" comprises household and similar waste. There is no indication about the share of waste from industry, commerce and offices similar to household waste, which is included in this item.

The first survey deals with municipal waste. The respondents to the enquiry are municipalities operating one or more landfill site. Up to now, there is no privately owned landfill. By use of a written questionnaire, data are gathered about the quantities of municipal waste, construction waste and non-hazardous industrial waste disposed. The sites for permanent storage of construction waste – usually not accepting any other type of waste - are included in this survey.

An additional characteristic of the survey is that it includes the names of the settlements using the reporting landfill installation. Combining this information with the official number of inhabitants in these settlements allows to calculate the total population served by the landfill site. The quantity deposited in the surveyed sites covers waste generation in an area, in which 75 per cent of the Bulgarian population are living.

The second survey is dedicated to industrial waste generation. The questionnaire is sent to the companies taking part in the survey on air pollution within the CORINAIR programme. The NSI elaborated a short waste list for collection of data on the generation of non-hazardous industrial

wastes, which allows publication of waste data in terms of 16 categories. Data on hazardous waste are collected by the MEW.

In the past, the companies reported the waste quantities generated and the place of disposal (on-site, at another industrial plant or at the municipal landfill site). The NSI did not face substantial methodological problems like non-response or low data quality as a result of non-availability of sufficient information at the waste generating industrial unit.

Since 1998, the official waste statistics are in a phase of transition. After the Limitation of the Harmful Impact of Waste on the Environment Act (LHIWEA), dated 18 September 1997, and its by-laws became effective during the period up to 1999, the basic conditions for waste statistics changed. As the waste law deals, among other topics, with waste treatment, processing and recycling of waste, the statistical definition of waste and the coverage of activities must be changed. From the point of data collection, the most important regulation provides that waste must be classified according to a waste list which is equivalent to the European Waste Catalogue (see Order no. RD-323, dated 10 August 1998, pursuant to Article 23 LHIWEA).

This new waste list consists of 643 items, each item identified by a 6-digit number. Within the list, 197 categories are classified as hazardous. 80 per cent of the waste categories are process-oriented (mainly production-oriented), the rest is more or less substance-oriented. The processes form the next hierarchical level (101, e-digit).

According to the waste law, the industrial waste producers are obliged to keep a record-book of generation, treatment and disposal. This legal request forces the companies to build up or improve their internal information system on waste. After some time of introduction, it can be expected that a detailed picture of the waste stream within the company will exist and be available to company management. In addition to data reporting, the companies have to provide an annual report on their internal waste management.

Similar regulations are to be applied by the operators of municipal landfills. The difference to the rule for industrial generators of waste is that municipalities should not classify the disposed waste quantities by type, in accordance with the new, official waste list, but should instead use a short list of waste types including four items.

6.3   Conclusions and recommendations

In general, the conditions for developing good waste statistics in Bulgaria are favourable, as the recent changes and specifications point into the direction of modern solutions. The general orientation for future work should therefore be to enlarge the existing system in a substantive direction, progressively providing a growing share of the information needed for purposes of waste policy and management. The statistical instruments for an advanced analysis regarding both the type of indicators needed and the rules for calculation of waste indices should be left to the time, when larger amounts of statistical data are available in this field.

The necessary knowledge and experience in techniques of advanced data collection and processing are available. They can be trusted to solve the many serious methodological questions that are encountered in the transition process, which reside primarily in the data collection process, applying sound statistical theory, and in the processing of data, needing modern information technology. The revision of data collection methods should also cover the elimination of redundancies, as they occur for example in relation to water data, which are collected from enterprises in similar form, but independently, by the NSI and the EEA (see Chapter 5). However, specific recommendations with regard to methodological issues do not seem to be necessary at this stage, except that it should not be overlooked that the solutions to methodological problems demand the commitment of substantial financial and staff resources.

Generation of waste

A complete picture of the generation of primary wastes can be obtained, but the calculation would require some changes in the data sources. They should permit a breakdown into a more limited number of waste categories. It is proposed to compile the quantity of industrial waste in 40 waste categories. This level of detail will meet most of the information needs of the public and policy-makers, as it would enable to indicate the main structure of wastes at the point of generation, i.e. at the beginning of the waste flow.

Household and similar waste. According to the definition given in the LIHWEA (Additional Provision, Art. 1, item 2), household waste includes waste from private households, small industry and the tertiary sector of the economy. The information will be provided by the operators of landfill sites providing the yearly household waste reports according to Art. 13 of Regulation No. 10 (on the Filling out of the Report and the Waste Management Information Documents, dated 6 November 1998). The form of this report asks for a further breakdown of the respective waste volume by origin: household, offices, commerce and industrial activity. For practical reasons – common use of dust-bins by households, offices and commerce, lack of differentiation in waste disposal fees for the various groups of generators – these details cannot be expected from the operators of landfill sites, nor from waste collectors.

The figures obtained will therefore be very rough estimates, and the information concerned could be obtained in a more reliable manner by using information from industry. The volume of waste similar to household waste which is generated by industry and delivered to municipal landfills should be deducted from the aggregate reported by industry and shown separately on their reporting forms. This figure should be supplemented by the volume of wasted paper and cardboard, glass, plastic and textile waste which is collected separately (for details see below).

Recommendation 6.1:
The annual statistical reporting by landfills should be simplified by eliminating the question on the origin of household or similar wastes.

Non-hazardous industrial waste. Article 7 of Regulation No. 10 imposes on industrial units a yearly report of generation, treatment and disposal of waste. It covers the industrial sectors mining and quarrying, manufacturing and energy. The reporting obligation starts at a waste generation of 100 kg per day. Types of waste have to be shown using the official waste list, and a distinction has to be made between generation inside the unit, and waste received from outside the unit.

These data allow to present the generation of industrial wastes in great detail. In the case of the energy sector, figures on the generation of cinder and ashes should be taken from another source, because these waste categories are not covered by the report form.

For statistical presentation, it is inappropriate to use the waste list at the detailed 6-digit level. Instead, a condensed version of 30 to 40 items should be elaborated. Solid and liquid wastes and sludges originating from pollution abatement facilities will have to be shown separately.

Recommendation 6.2:
A source of statistical information for the generation of cinder and ashes in energy transformation industries should be determined. A reduced classification of non-hazardous industrial wastes ·should be developed for statistical presentation of both generation and disposal of such wastes, including not more than 30 to 40 types of waste.

Hazardous industrial waste. Hazardous wastes from industrial processes are well documented, as are other industrial wastes. According to the requirements of Bulgarian legislation, hazardous wastes are fully controlled as all sources of generation are controlled regardless of the quantities produced.

An aggregation of the hazardous waste list is recommended similar to the proposal for industrial wastes.

Recommendation 6.3:
Statistical collection of data on the generation of hazardous waste should include provisions that enable satisfactory coverage of generation of waste oils in small repair shops. A reduced classification of hazardous industrial wastes should be developed for statistical presentation of both generation and disposal of such waste, including approximately 30 to 40 types of hazardous waste.

Construction waste. The source of information about generation of construction waste is the yearly report of landfill sites accepting this waste for disposal. In this case, the quantity of waste disposed must be considered as the total generated. The term 'construction waste' comprises a 2-digit-group of the waste list, and probably also soil and stones from construction sites. The respondents are not requested to provide a further breakdown.

Sludge from waste-water treatment. The information form filled in by industrial units includes data on sludge from on-site waste-water treatment facilities as a sub-category of primary waste. This picture will be completed by the amount of sludge generated in public waste-water treatment plants. Assuming that the household waste report mentioned above will not permit the

compilation of reliable data on this waste, the figures on sludge should be derived from a statistical survey of public waste-water treatment installations.

Recommendation 6.4:
A special statistical survey should be undertaken in order to obtain reliable information on generation of sludge from waste-water treatment.

Recycling

Recycling is a main item of waste management and a new topic for waste statistics. Recycling activities are concentrated in Bulgarian industries operating recycling facilities on-site. The reporting form for industrial waste contains information about quantities and type of waste for recycling, and the type of the recycling process installed. If the recovery activities are executed in another plant, the identification of this operator is also possible, so that double-counting may be avoided. In short, recycling activities in industry are well documented and the data make the calculation of recycling rates possible.

The information is limited to the input of recycling installations whereas the result of the process and the substitution of secondary for new materials remain unknown. This target of recycling should also be subject to statistical reporting.

After the collapse of the Sero-system, which was a State-owned recycling company, collecting metals, textiles, paper, plastics and glass for recycling, some collection of waste material has been established in the recent past by private companies. They are dealing with waste paper and cardboard, glass, textile and plastic waste, scrap metals and used automobile tyres, acting as wholesalers. Except for intermediate storage, the material collected is sold to domestic recovery facilities or exported. As these companies will also import waste material of that type, the balancing of the waste flow for recycling will become complicated without further information. According to the requirements of regulation N 10, those companies that recycle or reuse waste also need to report regularly on industrial and hazardous wastes (information cards).

It is doubtful whether manufacturing companies buying waste paper, glass or used tyres in the market as secondary raw material or fuel consider them as waste. Consequently, they might not report them on the waste form. Moreover, data on the input of imported secondary material are missing. It is recommended to study this field carefully and to design a special statistical survey when the result is negative.

Recommendation 6.5:
A special statistical survey should be envisaged for the recycling of waste. The use of recycled material may also require special data collection efforts.

Treatment

The treatment of waste prior to final disposal is considered a segment of waste management of growing importance. The technical processes applied to change the composition and quality of waste that may be considered here are: Incineration to reduce the content of pollutants, separation of emulsions, filtering, distillation, evaporation and de-watering, sedimentation and flocculation, oxidation, neutralization. At the present state of waste management, the equipment for these processes is installed mostly at the waste generator, who treats the own waste and, in some cases, is prepared to take over waste from other producers.

It is suggested to restrict the collection of such statistics to the input side of the installations. Obviously, this will limit the content of the final information, in so far as the effectiveness of the treatment measure is not shown. This objective cannot be achieved by statistical means, because the great variety of the chemical composition of the individual waste before and after treatment would make the standardization impossible, which is needed for statistical purposes.

The reports for production waste and for hazardous waste will comprise data on the treatment inside and outside the industrial unit. In order to avoid double-counting, the statistic should be confined to treatment on site. The input figures would thus cover waste volumes generated in the reporting unit and received from others.

Recommendation 6.6:
Statistics on waste treatment by type of treatment should be collected from the treatment installations only. The treatment types distinguished should be incineration, separation of emulsions, filtering, distillation, evaporation and de-watering, sedimentation and flocculation, oxidation, and neutralization.

Final disposal

The municipal landfill sites are the 'backbone' of final disposal. The operators hold data on the quantities of waste deposited, subdivided into the types "household waste", "construction waste", "industrial waste" and "hazardous waste", in accordance with their respective permits. The classification is quoted from the reporting book and must be assessed as an insufficient description of the waste items.

To be consistent with the set of data on waste generation, a similar grouping should be realized at the final disposal of wastes. The sources for such data are the information forms for production and for hazardous waste. Respondents have to indicate, among other things, the municipal landfill which they used for depositing each type of waste. Applying adequate data processing techniques, the figures of wastes collected from industry can be combined with the relevant data of municipal landfills. The result will be a breakdown of industrial wastes deposited in municipal landfills, by type. See Recommendation 6.1.

The second group of landfill operators are industrial units. The data provided by them comprise the quantities of waste by type at the 6-digit-level. The facilities should be classified as "landfill for industrial waste", "hazardous waste", "tailing pond", "pond for sludge" and "others".

Concerning the level of management in both the municipal and industrial landfills, the characteristics "barrier towards groundwater", "drainage of leachate" and "gas recovery" are sufficient. For municipal sites, the existence of "scales", a "control check-point" and a "fence" should be added.

Estimates say that, besides the 620 municipal landfill sites, approximately 800 dumping places are used, which are uncontrolled and lack any legal basis. Observing Regulation No. 10, the municipalities tolerating these sites will also have to fill in the information form on household waste. It is expected that, by this means, some information on these dumping grounds can be obtained.

Recommendation 6.7:
Statistics on waste disposal by industrial units acting as landfill operators should distinguish

between the different types of disposal operations: landfill for industrial waste, landfill for hazardous waste, tailing pond, pond for sludge, and other. Concerning the management of both municipal and industrial landfills, they should be classified as being equipped by barrier against groundwater, drainage of leachate, equipped for gas recovery. For municipal sites, the existence of scales, of a control check-point and of a fence should be additionally distinguished.

Transboundary movement of waste

The by-laws to the LIHWEA regulate licensing and movement of waste across the border, including reporting. The statistical figures will be provided by the MEW and should be added to the waste balance in an adequate way.

Organization of statistical work

The yearly information reports, ordered by Regulation No. 10, will cover the majority of data needed for waste statistics. Therefore it is obvious to use these administrative sources in order to reduce the response burden of the economic units involved. However, in the long term, growing concerns with response burden by industry to all types of administrative enquiries may require statistical surveys for an increasing number of information requirements.

The reports must be delivered to the responsible Regional Environmental Inspectorate (REI) and will form one part of their records for carrying out their supervisory activity. This raises the organizational question whether the REI or the NSI should elaborate the statistics on waste generation, recycling, treatment and disposal. Undoubtedly the staff of REI have the expertise to assess the validity of the declarations in the reports. On the other hand, the NSI has long experience in dealing with large data masses and can provide the hard- and software for data processing. It is hoped that the Executive Environmental Agency and the NSI will find an understanding on how to share the work load of establishing the new set of waste statistics in the most efficient way.

Chapter 7

MANAGEMENT OF THE REVISION OF PROTECTED AREAS

7.1 Existing area protection and its problems

Nature conservation and area protection

Protected areas today cover between 4.3 per cent and 4.5 per cent of the territory. General information on existing protected areas and their development is presented in Figure 7.1. The positive trend between 1991 and 1995 in the creation of protected areas seems currently stabilized. In 1999-2000, however, changes in the terminology of protected area and forest area categories resulted in re-categorizing and re-bordering processes that have still to be completed.

Figure 7.1: Categories, number and ownership of protected areas, 2000

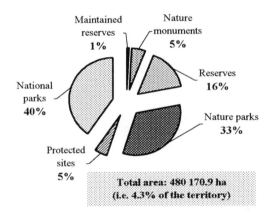

Type	Number	Ownership
Total	703	
Reserves	55 *	State exclusively
National parks	3	State exclusively
Nature monuments	475	State, municipal, private
Maintained reserves	35	State exclusively
Nature parks	10	State, municipal, private
Protected sites	125	State, municipal, private

* including 17 biosphere reserves

Source: Ministry of Environment and Waters.

In 1995, the MEW intended to protect 7.5 per cent of the national territory by the year 2000. Currently, protected forests or "forests of special purposes", represent about 8.3 per cent to 9.6 per cent of forest coverage. The coastal zone is protected by 12 protected areas that cover up to 65 per cent of the Bulgarian Black Sea coastline. In 1996-1997, the Committee on Forestry mapped the national zones where there was the greatest biodiversity. Protected areas cover a small part of these zones (see Figure 7.2).

During the last two years, the Bulgarian protected area system has been modernized considerably along with changes in land ownership. Figure 7.1 includes the status of ownership according to the various categories of protected areas. Private owners of protected areas are entrusted with new responsibilities regarding protection and conservation, for which management plans are being developed by the Ministry of Environment and Waters and the Ministry of Agriculture and Forestry. The 35 existing "Maintained Reserves" are of exclusive Stateownership, but those going to be designated and established in the future might be of State, municipal or private ownership. Their current number and total area are indicated in Figure 7.1. The Bulgarian land redistribution makes it clear that the agricultural lands, located within protected areas, should not be returned to their former owners.

In addition to the categories shown in Figure 7.1, the Bulgarian protected areas network since 1995 includes the new category "ecosystem sites" that in most cases have been incorporated into the existing

Figure 7.2: **Geographical mapping of high level biodiversity zones and protected areas**

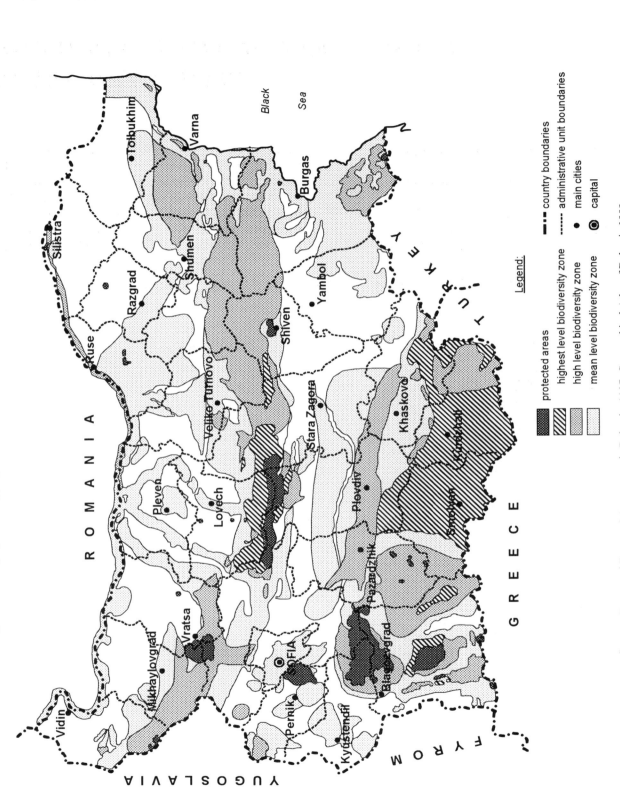

Source: Forest and Forestry Management in Bulgaria, 1997; Geographical Atlas of Bulgaria 1999.

protected areas system. 11 forests, 4 scrubs and grasslands, 7 rivers, 7 lakes, 2 coastal and marine areas, and 1 mountain area (bordering Greece) have thus been designated as representative ecosystem sites of importance at the European level. In general they are adequately protected (type "A" or "B" according to the Dobříš report), except for two cases classified as type "F" (not protected and under threat) - Lake Mandra and the Rhodopi Mountains. Recently, in relation to the birds and habitats directives, the MEW reported that 140 sites are qualified for protection.

Nature conservation in forests

Forest area represents 30.2 per cent of the Bulgarian territory, but has undergone noticeable overpatching. For example, during the last four years, the ratio between coniferous and broad-leaved high-stem forest area has changed substantially (Figure 7.3). In 1997-1998, the FAO declared that forest resources were increasing, due to afforestation programmes and cautious utilization.

Bulgaria has several natural areas of international importance, notably certain types of forest, high mountain grasslands, as well as areas of alpine vegetation. The forests include the only example of Pontic beech in Europe. Protected areas represent 8.3 per cent to 9.6 per cent of the forest total. There were no new protected forest areas (as part of the total protected areas network) created during 1997-2000, but a plan for enlarging forest areas has been developed.

Bulgarian forests function as ecological corridors for many animals. In 1999 some NGOs reported that during the war period in Yugoslavia the bear population in Bulgaria had temporarily increased and then decreased again thereafter, as an example of the functioning of the corridors and movements of animals therein. Wolf populations had behaved similarly.

Local forest industries use domestic wood to meet local demand for sawn-wood, panels, pulp and paper. Forests also shelter important non-wood forest products including wild animals, mushrooms, medicinal herbs and fruit. Annually, 700-1000 tonnes of wild herbs are exported, of which 50 per cent are collected in the mountains. The tendency has been increasing during the last few years.

Information about the next steps in the integration of Bulgaria into transfrontier European initiatives for forest protection and rehabilitation, and regarding forest certification initiatives (excluding joint monitoring), were not available at the time of the EPR Review Mission. Since 1986, however, Bulgaria has taken part in the international cooperative programme on monitoring of atmospheric pollution of forests. In 1998, 135 control plots were monitored, but Bulgaria is not represented in the initiative list of the forests certified by the Forest Stewardship Council. In 2000, some indirect action on the protection of forest ecosystems included protection from acidification, from garbage along tourist trails and the protection of medical plants, mushrooms, etc.

Figure 7.3: Bulgarian forests, 1955-2005

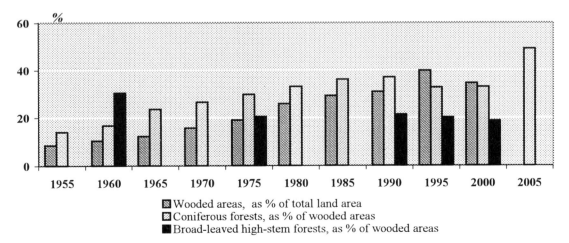

■ Wooded areas, as % of total land area
▨ Coniferous forests, as % of wooded areas
■ Broad-leaved high-stem forests, as % of wooded areas

Sources: Raev, Asan, Grozev, 1997; Committee on Forestry, 1997; SoE report 1997; Bojinov, 1998; Green Book 1998; 2000/2005: extrapolation.

The adaptation of existing legislation on forest management, and the development of new mechanisms for sustainable development involving the local population in decision-making, continue to be priorities for the Government.

Current problems in protected area management

Since the first EPR of 1995, the main risks and challenges for protected area management have changed. The dominating problem is the resource problem, i.e. lack of funds and lack of staff. Since 1995-1997, the situation has remained unfavourable. The annual expenses for protected areas from 1995 to 1998 fluctuated between 0.08 per cent and 0.6 per cent of the total environmental budget. The 1998 figures may have further decreased in 1999 (from 1.685 million to 0.857 million leva). In 1999, the National Nature Park Service managed protected areas in a way that did not correspond to recognized standards, and contrary to plans, the Directorate for National Parks was understaffed.

As a result, the legal protection goals could temporarily not be matched for reclassified or re-delimited protected areas, rendering earlier plans to increase the protected areas to 7.5 per cent of the national territory by the year 2000 impossible.

Other problems are related to changes in spatial planning, corresponding to privatization and economic transition. On the whole, conflicts of interest have become stronger. For example, the lakes and swamps along the Danube river have been drained with the exception of Srebarna Lake, which has UNESCO status, and numerous dams have been built. Along the Bulgarian Black Sea coast, the 130 km of beautiful wide beaches are one of the country's main tourist attractions and 65 per cent of the coastline is included in 12 protected coastal areas. Nevertheless, the European Union for Coastal Conservation (EUCC) calculated that between 1990 and 1998 natural dunes decreased by about 30 per cent. There are two wetlands of international importance (lakes Shabla and Srebarna) out of the five potential candidate sites identified in1993 for the Ramsar Convention. The Trigrad mixed forest of spruce and Austrian pine of 300 ha appears in the WWF European Forest Hotspots list.

All types of ecosystems outside protected areas are at present under serious human pressure. The National Biodiversity Conservation Programme

(NBCP) has identified a number of specific major threats to ecosystems (general approach): marine and coastal – 4, forest – 5, mountain (pasture) – 3, lowland (grass) – 3, agri-ecosystems – 6, inland water and wetland – 8. The existence of such threats of various kinds and origins shows the need to devise strategies to raise public awareness.

New farmers seriously impact on all components of the future Bulgarian segment of PEEN, a circumstance requiring education efforts among them. And while there is an intention to develop best agricultural practices in the future, so far there are no guidelines. For instance, woodland has recently been restituted, and some of the new owners (called "the arsonists") wanted to convert their property into agricultural land. There is also the problem of conservation of agricultural buffer zones near forests. Uncontrolled forest cutting is taking place for example in the Vitosha National Park. Cases of forest fire continue to occur due to firing of dry native grasses and stubble. Recultivation of 15,000 ha devastated in a recent fire on Mt. Sakar (Southeastern Bulgaria) is estimated to have cost about 10 million leva.

Problems of management of the Central Balkan territory and the Rila Mountain territories were investigated in details between 1994 and 1998 and reported in 2000 in the Bulgarian-Swiss Biodiversity Conservation Programme. Amongst the problems highlighted were the needed development of interdepartmental cooperation directed to improve ecotourism management, administration, recreation regulations, sustainable development of local communities, and the ecological safety of small dairy industries. Scientific research confirmed that pollution caused by local and transboundary sources was affecting the Central Balkans, including the highlands zone, hampering the certification of local dairy production as being of European Union quality.

There is no restriction on trading in animals not listed in the CITES Convention. In 1999, Bulgarian authorities identified some technical challenges concerning control of the trade in species of wild fauna and flora. Significant improvement of the legislation is required for the setting up of the control procedures, labelling, confiscation, etc. in connection with the trade in species. The problems could be solved partly through transposition of EU regulations and directives in this field. The adoption of the Law on Trade in Endangered Species, the Law on Biodiversity, the Hunting Law, and the Regulation on the development of plans for protected areas management will pave the way for transposition of additional EU regulations and directives, such as Regulations 3254/91/EEC and 338/97/EC, Directive 79/409/EEC and Directive 92/43/EEC. Full implementation is foreseen in three years at the latest.

A transitional period is needed for the preparation of national lists of protected habitats and species. The main challenges for the implementation of EU practices are the protection of wild birds outside protected areas, the strict protection of some species not yet protected, and the need for institutional strengthening of nature protection administrations at central and regional levels.

7.2   Strategies and policies for area protection

Development of an overall strategy

During the past decade, Bulgaria has progressively developed its objectives for nature conservation as a whole, in accordance with elements of the Pan-European Biological and Landscape Diversity Strategy (PEBLDS). Progress was slow concerning

the contribution to the Pan-European Ecological Network (PEEN). Box 7.1 presents the respective developments in a synoptic manner.

Improving the protected area network is one of the seven priority fields identified for immediate action and support in the 1998 first Report on Conservation of Biodiversity in Bulgaria. Science, legislation, education, ecotourism, conservation of the Black Sea Basin, and the Balkan Peninsula are the other priorities. Other initiatives have been added to improve territories and landscapes as requested under the 1999 Territorial Planning Bill.

Box 7.1 shows that, in the mid-nineties, the following sequence of management objectives for nature conservation and biodiversity protection undertaken on an informal basis, without the appeared: firstly the ratification of the Convention on Biodiversity (CBD), followed by the elaboration of the Biodiversity Conservation Strategy (BDCS), leading to orientation towards PEBLDS targets and finally joining the Pan-European Ecological Network (PEEN).

Box 7.1: Evolution of nature conservation policy and protected area management in Bulgaria, in relation to EU requirements

Early nineties:
- Situation begins to change regarding the legal framework and resource endowment of nature conservation efforts;
- A law on protected areas is adopted;
- An agency for management of protected areas is created, associated with the Ministry of Environment;
- A Nature Conservation Fund is established;
- Training and education programmes are elaborated.

Mid-nineties:
- The CBD is ratified and relevant legislation formulated;
- An action plan is produced under the Biological Diversity Conservation Strategy;
- Proper management of protected areas is secured by enhancing technical capacity;
- Nature damage from pollutants is monitored and evaluated;
- Sustainable practice in forestry and agriculture is developed, and rural tourism is promoted through pilot projects;
- Illegal hunting and forest degradation (from farm privatization) are sanctioned;
- Acceleration of the development of the necessary legal, institutional and planning mechanisms is declared an urgent requirement.

Late nineties:
- Regulations are developed, under the existing laws, for the establishment of management plans in the protected areas, exclusively of State property;
- Other regulations connected to the Protected Areas Law are developed;
- New laws like the Biodiversity Law are drafted;
- The Law on Herbs, and other laws concerning unprotected areas and connected to the EU directives (habitat, birds, etc.) are developed;
- Obligations under signed conventions are implemented, and the participation in further ecological conventions (Bonn Convention, etc.) is prepared;
- Complete harmonization of national nature conservation legislation with that of Europe is targeted, so that Bulgaria may accede to the European Union.

In addition, and in accordance with the results of the bilateral screening in July 1999, a series of objections are raised concerning regulations 338/97/EC, 348/81/EEC, 3254/91/EEC, and directives 83/129/EEC, 79/409/EEC, and 92/43/EEC. The Government's new report on implementing the programme BULGARIA-2001 declares strong intentions to transpose the EU environmental legislation, and to accelerate the corresponding cooperation.

Figure 7.4: Institutions responsible for the management of the six categories of protected areas

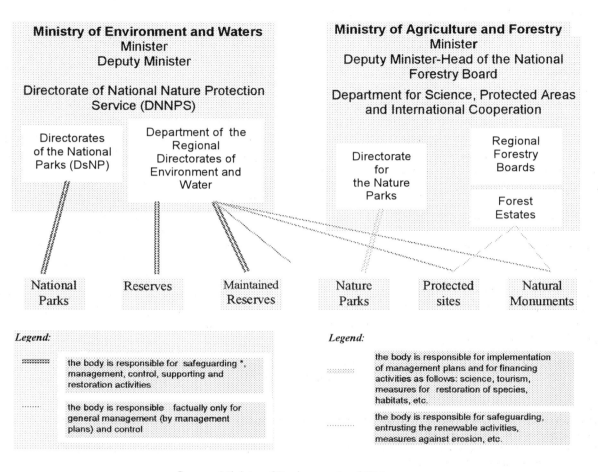

Source: Ministry of Environment and Waters

The MEW plays an important role in this process as a supervisor of CBD activities. New objectives concerning PEBLDS were formulated in the National Biodiversity Conservation Programme (NBCP), and published at the beginning of 2000. The 1999 budget, associated with NBCP, testifies to the leading role of the Ministry of Agriculture and Forestry, the Ministry of Environment and Waters, and the Ministry of Education and Science in the related management. In addition, the Ministry of Agriculture and Forestry is responsible for management of forest and agricultural lands of protected areas and sites, and for information about animals and plants. The Ministry of Economy begins to formulate its own objectives with regard to the sequence BDCS ⇨ PEBLDS ⇨ PEEN under the NBCP (See Figure 7.4 on institutional arrangements for protected areas management). During the final three years, the reclassification and revised delimitation of protected areas have continued and are planned to come to a conclusion during the following year and a half.

The new objectives relating to the implementation of the PEBLDS require permanent cooperation between all institutions involved in the CBD ⇨ BDCS ⇨ PEBLDS sequence, and into its further extension to the PEEN. In relation to PEBLDS, the three components of the ecological network (core areas, corridors, buffer zones) should be recognized early. Conservation will be secured through international instruments (particularly Natura-2000 and the Emerald Network) and policies (special programmes of national/regional authorities).

So far, in Bulgaria, a series of initiatives concerning the establishment or linkage to the PEEN has been support of any specific legal framework. Also, the PEBLDS spells out a series of thematic guidelines, which have not yet been taken into account by Bulgaria. An example is the development of management plans for transfrontier protected areas as required by the conclusions of the first International Symposium on the Pan-European Ecological Network (Paris, 1999).

Transposition of EU legal requirements

Bulgaria's most important legislative innovations related to PEEN are connected with EU directives. For the first time at the beginning of 2000, Bulgaria commented on regulations 338/97/EC, 348/81/EEC, 3254/91/EEC and directives 83/129/EEC, 79/409/EEC (birds), 92/43/EEC (habitat). Several regulations were transposed into the draft Law on Trade in Endangered Species that is scheduled for adoption in 2000. There is no restriction on trading in animals not listed in the CITES Convention. Significant improvement of the legislation is required for the setting up of the control, labelling, and confiscation procedures, but the competent authorities have already been designated.

Several of the EU Directives have been transposed into the Law on Protected Areas (reclassifying the network of protected areas), the Nature Protection Act, the Law on Hunting and the Law on Fisheries. The rest of the transposition procedure will be achieved in the Biodiversity Law scheduled for adoption in 2000, in the new Hunting Law adopted in 1999 and in the Regulation on Development of Plans for Protected Areas Management (adoption scheduled for 1999). The MEW plans to achieve full implementation of the Directives three years after their adoption.

The MEW report of 1999 on the implementation of the Birds and Habitats Directives states that about one third of potential ornithological SPA sites are already protected. Procedures are under way to protect other sites, but as this involves a considerable amount of time, the task may take up to three years to be completed. Thirty-four of 141 CORINE biotope sites, for which a database exists, are partly or fully ornithological sites in terms of the EU. Currently, 34 birds listed in the EU Directive are not protected in Bulgaria, and neither are some other widely represented bird species. The hunting of birds for sport is not prohibited. Six hunted wild animal species, such as the wolf, *canis lupus*, although listed in the Habitats Directive as strictly protected, are not protected in Bulgaria.

In contrast to other EU countries, Bulgaria implemented the Directives in a period of intensive reform of agriculture. It is expected that the land reform will contribute to increasing the density of the ecological protection infrastructure or ecological network. The original collectivization changed the appearance of the landscape, and the land reform will change it again. The process of restoring agricultural land to the former owners was completed in the period May 1997 to April 1998, when 4.05 million hectares of land were restituted to previous owners. Certificates of ownership were issued for 1.05 million hectares of agricultural land in a process that was completed in about half the time originally planned. Actually, the setting up of Special Protected Areas and Special Areas of Conservation (SPAs and SACs) that should be designated as an input in the EU network, are convenient instruments for rapid involvement of owners into a process of practical creation and mapping of the Bulgarian segment of PEEN.

Adaptation of biodiversity protection to European practices

The NPCB was adopted in 1999. The cost of the establishment and maintenance of the National Ecological Network up to 2003 was estimated at about one million leva. Eight main objectives were formulated. Among them were: (a) the re-categorization of existing protected areas, (b) the setting-up of new protected areas, (c) the modification of existing protected areas (regarding boundaries, regimes, etc.), and (d) the improvement of management arrangements in the Rila, Central Balkan, and Pirin national parks, and 70 other protected territories. Priority would be accorded to the aforementioned parks, the Vitosha and Stranja nature reserves, and 100 other protected territories.

Part of the future ecological network has already been officially designated. Two areas (Pirin National Park and the Sreburna Nature Reserve) are recognized as world natural heritage sites, under the 1972 Convention on the Protection of the World Cultural and Natural Heritage. Seventeen areas are listed as biosphere reserves under UNESCO's Man and Biosphere Programme and indicated on the EUROSIT map. Eight of them are of ornithological importance at the European level. Five wetlands of a total area of 2,803 ha are included in the Ramsar List. During the last eight years the Bulgarian Society for Bird Protection identified 50 important sites - amounting to about 7,000 km^2, or 6.3 per cent of the total national area and equivalent to the EU Bird Directive's Important Birds Areas. Definite measures proposed and other action taken protect only 76 per cent of these ornithological areas.

The five-year Action Plan on Conservation of Biodiversity (2000) is generally compatible with PEBLDS as regards core areas. A scheme of corridors and buffer zones, favouring mountain, forest and wetland habitats was drafted and is likely to be mapped and consolidated in accordance with Natura-2000 and Emerald Network requirements. Nevertheless, the process will require the further development of a relevant Geographical Information System (GIS, see below). Some other organizational developments were important for PESBLC. In 1999, Bulgaria, with the support of the Council of Europe, began a pilot project (together with Cyprus, Hungary and Romania) as a first step toward setting up the Emerald Network.

Management plans are implemented in the protected sites of "Veleka" and "The Mouth of Silistar" with the financial and expert support of the Government of Monaco. The development of management plans for large protected areas is being completed: the Rila and Central Balkan national parks, the Vitosha and Strandja nature parks, and the Srebarna reserve. Seven management plans for protected areas were prepared in the framework of the Bulgarian-Swiss Biodiversity Conservation Programme. Fundamental scientific materials on biodiversity of the Central Balkan and Rila were published in February-March 2000, as well as concepts on sustainable development and nature conservation in the Bulgarian part of the Rhodope Mountains – in 1999.

Further preparation of management plans for all protected areas (689) and putting them into practice are now a question of time and financial support for the NNPS Directorate, the Ministry of Environment and Waters and for their partners.

Development of transboundary protected areas

The creation of new protected areas, and the expansion of existing ones may be envisaged within the framework of the Forest Act and the Protected Areas Act, but there is at present no provision for transfrontier protected areas. New legislative approaches need to be devised within the PEEN strategy for the implementation of European practices. The following regional initiatives have been proposed:

Danube River Valley region. The basis would be the Protocol between the Ministry of Environment and Waters of the Republic of Bulgaria and the Ministry of Waters, Forests and Environmental Protection of Romania, signed in Sofia on 23 November 1999, and the Memorandum on cooperation concerning Danube nature conservation, including protected areas, signed on

16 November 1999. One of the points of interest of the Memorandum is the Sreberna Lake. Cooperative work could be directed primarily at monitoring the flooded forest. Further activities could be based on the first achievements of the EC international project for Bulgarian and Romanian ecological inspections of both banks of the Danube river, which included the creation of protected areas on Camadinu Island (Romania) and Ljulaka Island (Bulgaria). It may be possible to extend this work to the Rybarnitsa site.

Other improvements in local territorial planning could be sought to decrease poaching by local hunters and fishers and reinforce protection of the Red Data Book species. Regional cooperation projects, managed by UNDP, also concern the Danube and Black Sea protection. There is a new initiative on the creation of a Lower Danube Green Corridor and, in June 2000, the signing of a Declaration on cooperation between the Ministry for Environment and Waters of the Republic of Bulgaria, the Ministry of Environment and Territorial Planning of the Republic of Moldova, the Ministry of Waters, Forests and Environmental Protection of Romania and the Ministry of Environment and Natural Resources of Ukraine.

Western Balkan mountain region. During the past decade, the creation of a Park of Peace has been discussed on the basis of NGO initiatives in Bulgaria and Serbia.

Strandja mountain region. Initiatives in the nineties, by NGOs and scientists from Bulgaria and Turkey, aimed at the creation of a transfrontier protected area in the Strandja mountain region. Several years ago, the Institute of Zoology of the Bulgarian Academy of Sciences, stressed the importance of cooperative conservation of rare Mediterranean plants, animals and soils. The Agreement on Environmental Cooperation between the Government of the Republic of Bulgaria and the Government of the Republic of Turkey, signed in Ankara on 28 July 1997, would provide the basis for such action.

Belasica mountain region. Some Bulgarian NGOs (including the Wilderness Fund) proposed establishing the "Bekasite" protected area. This region is interesting because it is an area common to Bulgaria, the former Yugoslav Republic of Macedonia, and Greece, and could be linked with pan-European initiatives for the protection of trails of migratory bears. There is also a 1999 bilateral Agreement with Greece, under which common monitoring of the River Struma was organized with assistance from the PHARE programme.

Pirin and Rhodope mountain regions. The preceding proposal would be compatible with one seeking to enlarge protected areas in the Rhodope and Pirin mountain regions. Two NGOs (Wilderness Fund of Bulgaria, and "Arkturus" of Greece) are cooperating for the conservation of the bear population in the Mesta River Valley. The Ministry of Agriculture and Forests and MEW are exchanging ideas on enlarging the protected areas in the Eastern and Western Rhodope region.

Taking the WWF European Forest Hotspots into account, new projects could be launched, for example, in the Trigrad mixed spruce and Austrian pine forest. The restoration and protection of the Trigad forest would require an additional US$ 4,700 for the elaboration of a management plan, initial implementation activities, and awareness-raising measures with the local communities.

Bulgaria could take an active part in the initiatives on biodiversity conservation along the coastal zone of the Black Sea. The Azov-Black Sea ecological corridor for conservation of biodiversity (GEF project) developed in Ukraine could thus be extended to the south-west. In 1997, the CBD requested its Parties to develop Marine Protected Areas. Since then, PEEN has recommended that Thematic Guidelines on the issue be elaborated. Bulgaria could take these new initiatives into account along with the new IUCN - World Commission on Marine Protected Areas Initiative which has begun to develop further guidelines for protected marine areas.

Eco-tourism development

Governmental institutions and non-governmental organizations have developed elements of a potential national policy on ecotourism, within the framework of projects such as the ongoing GEF project on ecotourism in the Central Balkan National Park and Rila National Park, and the PREST project for planned development of tourism in the Pirin region.

Ecotourism is an important economic development option for Bulgaria, possibly adding to the weight of enlargement plans for protected areas. There are many examples of successful implementation of public awareness campaigns and development of tourism activities by the National Nature Park Service. The exhibition space in the "Rila" visitors'

centre in Panichishte is completed. The MEW provides funds to finance nature protection programmes on the media and the environmental "Planeta" programme on national television and the magazines "ECO", "Svyat", etc. Other programmes on local radio and television stations are funded from international projects.

The promotion of ecotourism is increasing, facilitated by the use of the Internet. Many possibilities are offered to visit protected sites and discover their biological treasures. The *Sofia City Info Guide* invites visitors to the Vitosha Mountains, Knyazhevo, Bojana, Dragalevtzy, Simeonovo, Bistritsa (the UNESCO World Heritage Conservation Area), Pancharevo, Gorna Banya, Bankya, and Pamporovo. The *SEARCH-BG* company demonstrates the effectiveness of Bulgarian Internet Resources, which now include *Ecology* and *Green Farms* pages. *ECO TOURS* provide vacation opportunities in the "Iskar" reserve. Bulgaria, through the *INFO-HUB* international service, offers bird-watch tours to the lake Atanasovsko reserve, Kaliakra reserve and Mt. Vitosha National Park.

Vital areas for birds have been identified and some measures taken to direct bird watching in a way that will favour tourism yet represent a minimal risk for birds and natural features. Most of the private tour operators establish contact with other key players (NGOs). The Bulgarian Society for the Protection of Birds cooperates with the major Bulgarian nature-tour operators. In the Bulgarian nature conservancy Dobrudja there is a project intended to promote ecotourism in Primorska Dobrudja.

Monitoring and other information for nature protection

To build a unifying and interactive network in Bulgaria during the initial phase of the PEEN remains an important effort. Beginning in 1997, with financial support from the PHARE programme, the Bulgarian National Bio-monitoring Programme was elaborated, and was finally published in 1999. The programme describes total network information requirements, encompassing protected areas and areas of prospective protection. It covers a series of 86 bio-parameters, 16 background control stations concerned with types of ecosystems and pollutants, 95 impact control stations for the estimation of industrial pollution, 18 sensitive phytomonitors and fungi to assess the reaction of the plant components of the ecosystems, and 50 sensitive zoomonitors (of invertebrate and vertebrate animal species and their communities) for the assessment of the animal components of the ecosystems. About 40 per cent of fresh water algae species found in the Central Balkan National Park are considered bioindicators.

In the year 2000, this monitoring network is expected to begin operating, although not under a fully effective regime, owing to the lack of finance, equipment and sufficient training of newly involved observers. Permanent cooperation with the Bulgarian Academy of Sciences is being recommended.

Since 1994, Bulgaria has been included in the CORINE Biotopes project, and 141 CORINE sites were designated up to 1995-1996. Nevertheless, this map requires revision, and new scientific materials and sources should be taken into account.

In 1999/2000, action was taken to develop a register of ecological and protected areas and a geo-referenced information system. The scheme was first announced in the 1998 National Report on Biodiversity Conservation, and then repeated in the MEW report on the BULGARIA-2001 programme. The GEF biodiversity database for the Central Balkan National Park was completed in 1998. Most of this information has been published in 379 scientific reports, but the data on 1,087 taxa has not been published. The GIS contributes data to the biodiversity database of the Rila National Park. It was developed and tested during 1996-1998, in the Autocad Map-2000^{TM} operating system of the AUTODESK Company. The biodiversity database stores information about 426 taxa of vascular plants, 92 mosses, 7 freshwater algae, 228 Macromycetes fungi, and 3,897 zoological taxa.

In 1998, Bulgaria presented its fundamental scientific data for the mapping of biodiversity across Europe. In most cases, the information dated from 1994-1996. Specialized information about numerous animal and plant groups was lacking, in particular with regard to the common animal species that inhabit agro-landscapes. The last three editions of the Bulgarian Green Book do not indicate relevant trends, in particular for hunted forest animals and game birds.

Financing protected areas

Protected areas receive only limited funding, from either national or international sources. As a result, a large number of proposals for enlarging protected areas exists but the implementation of such projects has been very slow. Econet and other transboundary protected area projects have been studied on a conceptual basis, but their financing is unclear.

A number of traditional economic instruments exist that are specific to nature protection and some new mechanisms were introduced for biodiversity conservation purposes. The Forest Act and the Protected Areas Act have introduced licensing of specific activities. Administrative fees are due for environmental impact studies, licenses, issuance of permits, destruction of endangered species, etc. The Protected Areas Act provides for visitor entrance fees to protected areas. It also introduced an annual fee paid by hotel owners, sports facilities, and stores located on the territory of protected areas. Pollution fines have been tripled in some protected areas, while in others, e.g. protected zones around drinking water reservoirs and water supply equipment, fines are doubled if pollution occurs. The fees are paid into the National Environmental Protection Fund and go to national and regional recipients. The revenue generating mechanisms adopted in 1999-2000 could help to encourage local involvement and lead to financial support for new conservation activities and operations.

7.3   Conclusions and recommendations

Bulgaria has succeeded in developing a convincing model for the modernization of its nature conservation policy framework and biodiversity protection practices. Starting from a biodiversity conservation strategy, an action plan was developed compatible with the Pan-European Strategy for Landscape and Biodiversity Conservation that will find its continuation in the Pan-European Ecological Network.

The above fundamental policy and management scheme is fully in line with the country's European Union accession plans. During the accession process, many of the problems in the implementation of the policy plan will be solved. At the same time, others will require particular attention. For example, the speed of implementation of those PEBLDS steps which are already implemented in most European countries will probably have to be increased, in particular those relating to the establishment of the Pan-European Ecological network (PEEN). In accordance with PEBLDS, the Bulgarian segment of the PEEN should be in place by 2005.

In general, the Bulgarian intention to reach the planned percentage of protected areas within three years is probably optimistic. In accordance with 79/409/EEC policy, SPAs will have to be designated officially as an input to the SPA network of the EU. The Directive 92/43/EEC sets out an implementation procedure that comprises an initial six-year period ending in 1998 (national draft input period). By May 1998 none of the Member States had submitted complete lists. At the end of the next six-year period, i.e. in 2004, the Member States should designate the SACs and provide adequate protective measures.

The challenges for the implementation of the Directives 79/409/EEC and 92/43/EEC are to increase the protection of wild birds which are presently outside the protected areas, ensure the strict protection of some species not yet protected at all in Bulgaria, and strengthen institutions for nature protection at central and regional levels. The situation requires the preparation of national lists of habitats and species needing protection, compatible with the Cadastre and GIS initiatives. Enforcement of new laws on hunting and on fishing is needed. Effective control according to these laws will require cooperation between the Regional Forestry Boards (operating under the Ministry of Agriculture and Forestry) and the National Natural Parks Service (of the Ministry of Environment and Waters).

The ongoing transposition of PESBLC and PEEN philosophy and terminology into the environmental laws will underline the importance of the key elements, the "transboundary protected areas", "ecological corridors", SPAs and SACs. However, other transboundary infrastructure projects like highways, railways, telecommunications, oil pipelines, power transmission lines etc., will create concerns for nature protection. In this regard, all current pan-European achievements in the establishment of ecological corridors across engineering constructions should be studied and, where possible, used as examples. To this end, the MEW should cooperate with all relevant institutions and NGOs, focusing on questions connected with globally threatened species (GTS actions), to prepare action plans for inclusion in national legislation, under the terms of Article 14 of the Bern Convention.

Further regulations need to be adopted related to the Protected Areas Act, including guidelines for the management of the protected areas of exclusive State property, guidelines for the functions and structure of the Directorates of the National Parks, a regulation for the development of management plans of protected areas (including forestry elements), a regulation on admission fees for protected areas and forests, as well as on payments for compensating damage caused to protected areas. Specific requirements should be developed in the bills for transboundary protected areas and for the protection of the biosphere.

Finally, Bulgaria's richness in terms of biodiversity makes the country a sort of island on the biodiversity map of Europe. The Ministry of Environment and Waters should determine priorities among the large number of well-developed projects included in the National Biodiversity Conservation Programme, possibly after some programme revision. Some of them have been mentioned in the National Report on Biological Diversity Conservation in Bulgaria. High-priority regions for new or expanded protected areas are the Rhodope Mountains, the Black Sea coast, Strandja Mountains, areas surrounding and connecting the existing national parks in the Rila, Pirin, Vitosha, and Stara Planina Mountains, and the valley of the Strouma river. It is suggested that increased international cooperation for biodiversity protection in the country be sought, through projects that could involve collaborative scientific research on the biogeography and biological diversity of the Balkan Peninsula, the preparation of Balkan-wide Red Data Books, etc.

Recommendation 7.1:
The unified administration of the sequence Biodiversity Conservation Strategy ⇒ Pan-European Strategy for Landscape and Biodiversity Conservation ⇒ Pan-European Ecological Network (including protected areas and objects) should be continued. The EU accession process should serve as a coordinating framework for all required legal and managerial improvements (including with regard to the obligations under environmental protection conventions). Priorities should be set among the measures proposed in the National Biodiversity Conservation Programme.

Due to economic difficulties in 1996-1997, monitoring of biodiversity was conducted for only some national parks and reserves. There is a lack of information concerning development trends of many species, above all the commoner species. The evaluation of this sector of interest should be accelerated, being particularly important for agricultural lands and forests and neighbouring protected areas.

The National Nature Protection Service is not operating on the basis of full information on protected areas. The development of a relevant information network including monitoring is regarded as a priority, together with the development of the GIS and a register of ecological and protected areas. Due to new fines, for example for herb and mushroom gathering and grazing in protected areas, which the Cabinet approved in 1999, and other regulations regarding the use of nature resources in buffer zones and in protected areas, new information will be required by the National Natural Protected Service. It is also necessary to foresee the inclusion of a protected areas component in the National Programme for the Adoption of the EU Common Acquis in the field of Statistics, which is under development.

The National Nature Protection Service should implement existing projects and develop new management and business plans, where possible within the framework of international cooperative projects for protected areas (e.g. the Central Balkans, Pirin, Silistar, etc.). A second priority for the Service should be the continuation of the development of a methodology aimed at evaluating the success of protecting biodiversity inside as well as outside the protected areas, with the purpose of disseminating conclusive information to land users. Thirdly, the Service should also continue the development of a methodology for assessing the economic value of biodiversity.

Exchanging bio-monitoring information should be considered an important preparatory measure for the creation of GIS and cadastre components, as well as forest certification components, including those relevant for the sequence BDCS ⇨ PEBLDS ⇨ PEEN. Materials already available could be used as such or updated. The publication and dissemination of unpublished scientific material from the nineties on animals and plants is highly desirable, as it would be helpful for the linkage of the Biodiversity Conservation Strategy and the PEBLDS.

The category of transboundary protected area does not exist so far in Bulgarian legislation. Relevant approaches need to be developed as pilot projects in new legislation preparing the PEEN implementation process, using current European experience (for example, that of the Czech Republic and Germany). Moreover, as biosphere reserves are not included as a special category in the legislation, it is not yet possible to enlarge biosphere reserves in transboundary regions, as has

been done in the Carpathian Region and the Danube Delta.

Recommendation 7.2:
The compilation and publication of information on protected areas and on aspects of biodiversity protection in adjacent areas should be improved. Such information should facilitate revision of legal instruments, enable decisions to be made in the event of conflicts over land use, and promote trans-frontier initiatives in the area of nature management.

As Bulgaria has recently taken steps to promote ecotourism, the adoption of a national policy on ecotourism and the integration of ecotourism into municipal and regional planning processes, environmental assessments, and environmental education programmes are required. At present, there is virtually no cooperation between the Ministry of Economy and the MEW in this regard (see Chapter 1). Internet information sources are being developed, but are not properly monitored. In March 2000, the Bulgarian report on the state of the environment in 1997 presented on the EIONET Internet site contained no information on protected areas, but included information about soil, water and air. Only the Sreberna Reserve and the Pirin National Park have their own web pages.

The cooperation of all interested parties in the NBCP needs to receive constant attention. Cooperation between the Ministry of Environment and Waters and the Ministry of Economy is an important priority along with cooperation with tourism firms, which began to advertise protected areas independently. The process will require the closer cooperation of all parties involved in the National Biodiversity Conservation Programme, including its PEBLDS component. The further unification of the nature management administration is an important part of the process, together with further unification of legislation.

Recommendation 7.3:
The cooperation between the Ministry of Environment and Waters and the Ministry of Economy should be improved, as it should with the companies that have begun to disseminate information on protected areas or the profitable use of protected areas. The scheme should promote the development of a fully coordinated policy on ecotourism, by guiding the development of tourism concepts at national, regional and local levels, as well as the publication of reliable and harmonized information on protected areas.

ANNEXES

Annex I

SELECTED ECONOMIC AND ENVIRONMENTAL DATA

Selected economic data

	Bulgaria
TOTAL AREA *(1 000 km^2)*	110.9
POPULATION	
Total population, **1998** *(100 000 inh.)*	82.30
- % change (**1993-1998**)	-2.71
Population density, **1998** *(inh./km^2)*	74.21
GROSS DOMESTIC PRODUCT	
GDP, **1998** *(US$ billion)*	12.26
- % change (**1993-1998**)	14.21
per capita, **1998** *(US$ per capita)*	1.470.38
INDUSTRY	
Value added in industry, **1998** *(% of GDP)*	25.5
Industrial output	-29.82
- % change (**1993-1998**)	
AGRICULTURE	
Value added in agriculture, **1998** *(% of GDP)*	18.7
Agricultural output	
- % change (**1993-1998**)	...
ENERGY SUPPLY	
Total supply, **199.** *(Mtoe)*	...
- % change (**199.-199.**)	...
Energy intensity **199.** *(toe/ US$ 1 000)*	...
- % improvement (**199.-199.**)	...
Structure of energy supply, **199.** *(%)*	...
- Coal	...
- Oil and oil products	...
- Gas	...
- Others	...
ROAD TRANSPORT	
Road traffic volumes, **199.**	
- *million veh.-km*	...
- % change (**199.-199.**)	...
- per capita *(1 000 veh.-km/inh.)*	...
Road vehicle stock, **1998**	
- 10 000 vehicles	211.36
- % change (**1993-1998**)	20.19
- private cars per capita **1998** *(veh./1 000 inh.)*	219.84

Sources: UNECE and National Statistics

Selected environmental data

	Bulgaria
LAND	
Total area **1998** *(1 000 km^2)*	110.9
Protected areas **1998** *(% of total area)*	4.42
Nitrogenous fertilizer use. **199.** *(tonne/km^2 arable land)*	...
FOREST	
Forest area *(% of land area)*	3.4
Use of forest resources (harvest/growth) % **199.**	...
Tropical wood imports *(US$/inh.)*	...
THREATENED SPECIES	
Mammals *(% of known species)*	...
Birds *(% of known species)*	...
Freshwater Fish *(% of known species)*	...
WATER	
Water withdrawal *(% of gross annual availability)* **199.**	...
Fish catches *(tonnes)*	...
Public waste water treatment *(% of population served)* **199.**	37.5
AIR	
Emissions of sulphur oxides. **1997** *(kg/inh.)*	165.80
Emissions of sulphur oxides. **199.** *(kg/US$ 1 000 GDP)*	...
Emissions of nitrogen oxides, **1997** *(kg/inh.)*	27.30
Emissions of nitrogen oxides, **199.** *(kg/US$ 1 000 GDP)*	...
Emissions of carbon dioxide, **199.** *(tonne/inh.)*	...
Emissions of carbon dioxide. **199.** *(tonne/US$ 1 000 GDP)*	...
WASTE GENERATED	
Industrial waste *(kg/US$ 1 000 GDP)* **1998**	2,486.15
Municipal waste *(kg/inh./day)* **1998**	1.06
Nuclear waste *(tonnes)* **1998**	-
NOISE	
Population exposed to leq > 65 dB (A) *(million inh.)* **199.**	...

Sources: UNECE and National Statistics

Annex II

SELECTED BILATERAL AND MULTILATERAL AGREEMENTS

Worldwide agreements as of 1 January 2000			Bulgaria
1949	(GENEVA) Convention on Road Traffic	y	R
1957	(BRUSSELS) International Convention on Limitation of Liability of Owners of Sea-going Ships	y	
1958	(GENEVA) Convention on Fishing and Conservation of Living Resources of the High Seas	y	
1963	(VIENNA) Convention on Civil Liability for Nuclear Damage	y	R
1969	(BRUSSELS) Convention on Civil Liability for Oil Pollution Damage	y	
	1976 (LONDON) Protocol	y	
1969	(BRUSSELS) Convention relating to Intervention on the High Seas in Cases of Oil Pollution Casualties	y	R
1971	(RAMSAR) Convention on Wetlands of International Importance especially as Waterfowl Habitat	y	R
	1982 (PARIS) Amendment	y	R
	1987 (REGINA) Amendments	y	
1971	(GENEVA) Convention on Protection against Hazards from Benzene (ILO 136)	y	
1971	(BRUSSELS) Convention on the Establishment of an International Fund for Compensation for Oil Pollution Damage	y	
1972	(PARIS) Convention on the Protection of the World Cultural and Natural Heritage	y	R
1972	(LONDON) Convention on the Prevention of Marine Pollution by Dumping of Wastes and Other Matter	y	
1973	(WASHINGTON) Convention on International Trade Endangered Species of Wild Fauna and Flora 1983 (GABORONE) Amendment	y	R
1973	(LONDON) Convention for the Prevention of Pollution from Ships (MARPOL)	y	R
	1978 (LONDON) Protocol (segregated balast)	y	R
	1978 (LONDON) Annex III on Hazardous Substances carried in packaged form	y	R
	1978 (LONDON) Annex IV on Sewage	y	R
	1978 (LONDON) Annex V on Garbage	y	R
1974	(GENEVA) Convention on Prevention and Control of Occupational Hazards caused by Carcinogenic Substances and Agents (ILO 139)	y	
1977	(GENEVA) Convention on Protection of Workers against Occupational Hazards from Air Pollution, Noise and Vibration (ILO 148)	y	
1979	(BONN) Convention on the Conservation Migratory Species of Wild Animals	y	
	1991(LONDON) Agreement Conservation of Bats in Europe	y	
	1992 (NEW YORK) Agreement ASCOBANS	y	
1982	(MONTEGO BAY) Convention on the Law of the Sea	y	S

Source: UNECE and Bulgaria.

     y = in force; S = signed; R = ratified

Worldwide agreements *(continued)*

Year	Agreement	In force	Status
1985	(VIENNA) Convention for the Protection of the Ozone Layer	y	R
	1987 (MONTREAL) Protocol on Substances that Deplete the Ozone Layer	y	R
	1990 (LONDON) Amendment to Protocol	y	
	1992 (COPENHAGEN) Amendment to Protocol	y	
	1997 (MONTREAL) Amendment to Protocol		
1986	(VIENNA) Convention on Early Notification of a Nuclear Accidents	y	R
1986	(VIENNA) Convention on Assistance in the Case of a Nuclear Accident or Radiological Emergency	y	R
1989	(BASEL) Convention on the Control of Transboundary Movements of Hazardous Wastes and their Disposal	y	R
1990	(LONDON) Convention on Oil Pollution Preparedness, Response and Cooperation	y	
1992	(RIO) Convention on Biological Diversity	y	R
1992	(NEW YORK) Framework Convention on Climate Change	y	R
	1997 (KYOTO) Protocol		S
1994	(VIENNA) Convention on Nuclear Safety		R
1994	(PARIS) Convention to Combat Desertification		
1998	(ROTTERDAM)Convention on the Prior Informed Consent Procedure for Hazardous Chemicals and Pesticides in International Trade		

Source: UNECE and Bulgaria.

y = in force; S = signed; R = ratified

	Regional and subregional agreements as of 1 January 2000		Bulgaria
1950	(PARIS) International Convention for the Protection of Birds	y	S
1957	(GENEVA) European Agreement - International Carriage of Dangerous Goods by Road (ADR)	y	
1958	(GENEVA) Agreement - Adoption of Uniform Conditions of Approval and Reciprocal Recognition of Approval for Motor Vehicle Equipment and Parts.	y	
1968	(PARIS) European Convention - Protection of Animals during International Transport	y	
	1979 (STRASBOURG) Additional Protocol	y	
1969	(LONDON) European Convention - Protection of the Archeological Heritage	y	R
1976	(BARCELONA) Convention - Protocol - Mediterranean Sea against Pollution	y	
	1976 (BARCELONA) Protocol - Dumping	y	
	1976 (BARCELONA) Protocol - Co-operation in Case of Emergency	y	
	1980 (ATHENS) Protocol - Land-based Sources Pollution	y	
	1982 (GENEVA) Protocol - Special Protected Areas	y	
	1994 (MADRID) Protocol against pollution from exploration/exploitation		
1979	(BERN) Convention - Conservation European Wildlife & Natural Habitats	y	R
1979	(GENEVA) Convention - Long-range Transboundary Air Pollution	y	R
	1984 (GENEVA) Protocol - Financing of Co-operative Programme (EMEP)	y	R
	1985 (HELSINKI) Protocol - Reduction of Sulphur Emissions by 30%	y	R
	1988 (SOFIA) Protocol - Control of Emissions of Nitrogen Oxides	y	R
	1991 (GENEVA) Protocol - Volatile Organic Compounds	y	S
	1994 (OSLO) Protocol - Further Reduction of Sulphur Emissions	y	S
	1998 (AARHUS) Protocol on Heavy Metals		S
	1998 (AARHUS) Protocol on Persistent Organic Pollutants		S
	1999 (GOTHENBURG)Protocol to Abate Acidification, Eutrophication and Ground-level Ozone		S
1991	(ESPOO) Convention - Environmental Impact Assessment in a Transboundary Context	y	R
1992	(HELSINKI) Convention - Protection and Use of Transboundary Waters and International Lakes	y	S
	1999 (LONDON) Protocol for Waters and Health		S
1992	(HELSINKI) Convention - Transboundary Effects of Industrial Accidents	y	R
1992	(BUCHAREST) Convention - Protection Black Sea Against Pollution	y	R
1993	(LUGANO) Convention - Civil Liability for Damage from Activities Dangerous For the Environment		
1994	(LISBON) Energy Charter Treaty		
	1994 (LISBON) Protocol on Energy Efficiency and Related Aspects		
1994	(SOFIA) Convention on Cooperation for the Protection and Sustainable Use of the Danube River		S
1998	(AARHUS) Convention On Access to Information, Public Participation in Decision-making and Access to Justice in Environmental Matters		S

Source: UNECE and Bulgaria.

y = y = in force; S = signed; R = ratified

SOURCES

Personal authors

1. Dick van der Zee - Land reform in Bulgaria: what will change? / Ecological and landscape consequences of land use change in Europe. (Edited by Rob.H.G.Jongman.) Tilburg, The Netherlands, 1995, pp. 367-385.
2. Popov A., Deltshev Ch., Hubenov Z. Invertebrate fauna – High Mountain Treeless Zone of the Central Balkan National Park. Biological Diversity and Problems of its Conservation. Bulgarian-Swiss Biodiversity Conservation Programme, 2000, 339-417 pp.
3. Vitkova A., Evstatieva L. Biodiversity of Medical Plants in the Rila National Park - Biological Diversity of the Rila National Park. (Managing editor: Marieta Sakalian.) ARD. Inc., USAID, 2000, 79-117 pp.
4. Webster R.,.Gray T., Jonson R. Partnerships for Sustainable Enterprise Growth. 21st Century Vision for USAID and its partners in Eastern Europe and the New Independent States. USAID. July, 1999.
5. Andrienko T.L. European approaches to creation of transboundary protected areas /Transboundary protected areas in Ukraine (authors' team). (Edited by T. Andrienko.) Kyiv, 1998, pp.13-15 – in Ukrainian.)
6. Kostadinova I. The national parks – pride or problem for Bulgaria? Sites of ornithological importance: Information bulletin of the Bulgarian Society of Protection of Birds #12, November, 1999, pp. 1-4 – in Bulgarian
7. Spiridonov G. Bulgaria – an Example of National Biodiversity Conservation Strategy : Workshop on Practical Implementation of Conservation on Biological Diversity, 25-27 June, 1996, Lessidren.
8. Roumen Avramov. Currency board et stabilté macroéconomique: le cas de la Bulgarie, revue de l'OFCE n° 72, janvier 2000.

Material from Bulgaria

1. Biological diversity of the Central Balkan National park. (Managing editor: Marieta Sakalian.) ARD Inc., USAID, 2000, 616 pp.
2. Biological Diversity of the Rila National Park. (Managing editor: Marieta Sakalian.) ARD. Inc., USAID, 2000, 648 pp.
3. Biosphere Reserve "Sreberorna" as a key object of the European Ecological Network. Material of seminar 25-26 September, 1999, Vetren. BSPB, 1999, 24 pp. in Bulgarian.
4. Bulgaria's Biological Diversity: Conservation Status and Needs Assessment. Volumes I and II/ 1998.Curt Meine, ed/ Washington. D.C.: Biodiversity Support Programme/ ISBN: 1-887531-21-1, 839 pp.
5. Conception and Structure of the Law on Biodiversity: Manuscript of the NNPS/MEW, 29 pp. November 22, 1999 – in Bulgarian.
6. Far from the Commotion of the West: Come and Enjoy Orpheus' Lyre. The Bulgarian Part of the Rhodope Mountains: Concepts for Sustainable Development and Conservation. (Editor – Hristo Nikolov, translator Dessislava Krusteva, designer – Lubomir Andreev.) Green Balkans, Plovdiv, 1999, 64 pp.
7. Forests and forestry management in Bulgaria. Edition of the Forestry Committee of the Ministerial Council of Republic of Bulgaria/ Editor Ivan Kostov. Sofia: K&M, 1997, 119 pp. – in Bulgarian.
8. High Mountain Treeless Zone of the Central Balkan National Park. Biological Diversity and Problems of its Conservation. Bulgarian-Swiss Biodiversity Conservation Programme, 2000, 562 pp.
9. Important Bird Areas in Bulgaria. Compiled by Irina Kostadiniva. Sofia: BSPB, 1997, 176 pp. - in Bulgarian.)
10. Information of the NNNP of MEW and MAF on results of calculation of hunting species in 1994-1998 and about percentage of hunting species in protected areas. Manuscript page of April, 14, 2000.
11. Institute of Zoology. BAS, Sofia, 1998, 60 pp.
12. National Biomonitoring Programme of Bulgaria/ BG9310-04-03-01/EU Programme: Phare/ Express And Long Term Methods For Biological Monitoring. Compilers and science editors: Ass.Prof.Dr. D. Peev, Prof.Dr.S.Gerasimov. Sofia: GEA-Libris, 1999, 240 pp. – in Bulgarian).
13. Preliminary proposals of the Protected Areas Department of the Committee on Forestry on prospective planning of the activity: CF/MAF, 2 pp. Manuscript of April, 2000 – in Bulgarian.
14. Proposal on financing of themes concerning conservation of biodiversity on 2000 and prospective : Manuscript of the NNPS/MEW, 6 pp. April, 2000 – in Bulgarian.
15. Protected area " The Veleka River Delta". Protected Area "Silistar". Managem,ent plan. (Under support of the Monaco Principality.) Sofia, 2000, 90 pp. in Bulgarian.
16. Report on Protected Natural Objects of 1998, NNPS/MEW, 08.01.1999 – in Bulgarian.
17. Report on Protected Natural Objects of 1999 (draft): NNPS/MEW, 2000 – in Bulgarian.
18. The Law on the Amendment and Supplements to the Protected Areas Law (Decree #84 of March 22, 2000) - Derzaven Vestnik 28, 2000. – in Bulgarian.
19. The National Biodiversity Conservation Plan. MEW, UNDP, GEF, Sofia, 2000, 59 pp.
20. The Nature Protection Law (of 1967, amended in - 1969, 1977,1978,1982,1988,1991,1997,29.01.1988,11.11.1988) – in Bulgarian

21. The Protected Areas Law (Decree #392 of 1998) – Derzaven Vestnik 133, November 11, 1998. – in Bulgarian.
22. The Report on the State of Environment in 1997 in the Republic of Bulgaria. Annual bulletin on 1997. National Center on Environment and Sustainable Development/ MEW. Sofia, 1999, 103 pp. - in Bulgarian.
23. The Report on the State of Environment in 1997. Green Book The Republic of Bulgaria. Ministry's Council. 108 pp. - in Bulgarian.
24. The Report on the State of Environment in 1998. Green Book The Republic of Bulgaria. Ministry's Council. Sofia, 2000, 102 pp. - in Bulgarian.
25. Up-to-dated table on the current situation with the protected areas in Bulgaria: Manuscript of the NNPS/MEW, April, 2000 – in Bulgarian.
26. Geographical Atlas for 10 class. (Editor – Gloria Dzadzaeva). Cartography, EOOD, Sofia, 1999, 63 pp. – in Bulgarian.
27. Strategy for Integrated Water Management in Bulgaria, Ministry of Environment and Waters, Sofia, 1997.
28. Bulgarian Waste Management Legislation, Ministry of Environment and Waters, Sofia, 1999.
29. National Waste Management Programme, Ministry of Environment and Waters, Sofia, 1999.
30. Periodic reports on National Environmental Fund, Ministry of Environment & Water/Bulgaria.

Regional and international organizations and institutions

1. Environmental Performance Reviews - Bulgaria, CCET/OECD, 1996
2. CIP: Facts&figures on Europe's biodiversity – state and trends 1998-1999. Ben C.W. Delbare (ed.), Tilburg: European Centre for Nature Conservation, 1998. 115 pp. (Technical Series ISBN 90-802482-7-4).
3. Europe's Environment: Statistical Compendium for the Dobřiš assessment. Luxembourg.: Office for Official Publications of the European Communities. 1995 – 455 pp.
4. T-PVS(97) 15 - Convention on the Conservation of European Wildlife and Natural Habitats/ Group of Experts on Conservation of Birds. Izmir, Turkey, 5-8 May, 1997, 123 p.
5. Partnerships for Sustainable Enterprise Growth. 21st Century Vision for USAID and its partners in Eastern Europe and the New Independent States (prepared by R.Webster, T.Gray, R.Jonson), July, 1999, 45 pp.
6. UNDP Development Cooperation Report 1998 - Bulgaria. Published September 1999
7. Project briefs, World Bank's Investment Program in Bulgaria, April 2000
8. The Business Handbook - Bulgaria, Deloitte & Touche, February 1996
9. Guidelines to investors in environmental projects, Ernst & Young/Phare, 1996
10. News items and web sites
11. Bansko - Bulgaria - - Ski Resorts SkiResorts.com Bansko -http://www.skiresorts.com/WORLD/Bulgaria/Bansko
12. Bern Convention News Web site, 2000. #2, July 1999 - http://www.nature.coe.int/english/cadres/berne.htm
13. BluLink Web page - http://www.bluelink.net- information of 10.03.2000
14. Bulgaria Biodiversity Project (1995-1998) Web site, 2000 http://www.ardinc.com/ardinc/projects/bulgaria/bulgaria.htm
15. Bulgaria Internet Resources Web site, 2000 – Environment and Nature, Ecology and farming in Bulgaria – in Bulgarian- http://www.search.bg/bin/c?_id-73
16. COP-5 ENB Vol. 09 No. 158.
17. Central Laboratory of General Ecology/ CLGE Web site, 2000.
18. European Environment Information and Observation NETwork (EIONET) Web page -http://www.eionet.eu.int/docu/soe.htm
19. European Forest Hotspots – WWF Web site – Hotspots Forest Profile/Bulgaria - Forest Futures (Tom Gardner and Robert Engelman) - Online report by SealRock Design & Communications -http://www.panda.org/forests4life/hotspots/med/index2.html
20. Forests Certified by FSC-Accredited Certification Bodies - DOC. 5.3.3 – Web site- http://www.panda.org/forests4life/frame_mainbgr.htm: information of April, 30, 2000
21. GEF Web site, 2000. Guidelines for additional funding of biodiversity enabling activities (expedited procedures), February 2000
22. Government of the Republic of Bulgaria Web site, 2000. (ПРАВИТЕЛСТВО НА РЕПУБЛИКА БЪЛГАРИЯ Web site – in Bulgarian and in English.) http://www.bulgaria.govrn.bg/bg/index.html
23. Lonely Planet - Destination Bulgaria - Web site, 2000 -http://www.lonelyplanet.com/dest/eur/bul.htm
24. National Statistical Institute Web site - http://www.nsi.bg
25. Natural Resource Aspects of Sustainable Development in Bulgaria http://www.un.org/esa/agenda21/natlinfo/countr/bulgaria/natur.htm#forests
26. Population Action International Web site, 1999 -http://www.populationaction.org/why_pop/forest/forest_index.htm
27. Ramsar Country Profiles: Bulgaria – http:/www.ramsar.org/profiles_bulgaria.htm
28. USAID CP FY2000:Bulgaria - http://www.info.usaid.gov/pubs/cp2000/eni/bulgaria.html
29. World Conservation Monitoring Centre Web site, 2000. 1996-Global Protected Areas Summary Statistics - http://www.wcmc.org.uk/protected_areas/data/summstat.html